EPIC TO EPIGRAM

EPIC TO EPIGRAM

An Anthology of Classical Verse

Re-Versed by Peter Hadley

With Foreword by Sir Jeremy Morse
(President of the Classical Association, 1989-90)

Bristol Classical Press

In retrospective gratitude to
those who guided my classical studies:

C.A. Browne

R.L. Arrowsmith
C.H. Blakiston
B.W.T. Handford
W.M. Howitt

Cyril Bailey
J.G. Barrington-Ward
D.L. Page

Stanley Casson
R.H. Dundas
R.P. Longden

First published in 1991 by
Bristol Classical Press
an imprint of
Gerald Duckworth & Co. Ltd.
The Old Piano Factory
48 Hoxton Square, London, N1 6PB

A catalogue record for this book is available from the British Library

ISBN 1-85399-195-3

Printed and bound in Great Britain by Booksprint, Bristol

Contents

FROM THE LATIN

Foreword

by Sir Jeremy Morse
President of the Classical Association, 1989-90

'Far on the ringing plains of windy Troy', 'Arms and the man I sing', 'They told me, Heraclitus, they told me you were dead', 'I do not love thee, Dr Fell': echoes of Homer and Virgil, Callimachus and Martial, of Greek and Latin epic and epigram, come drifting down to us through our English poetry. And so much else besides: tragedy, comedy and idyll; lyric, ode and satire; Sophocles, Aristophanes, Theocritus, Catullus, Horace, Juvenal. The great fount of classical Greek poetry, and the equally important derivative stream of Latin poetry, still flow through the modern poetry of the Western world.

Allusion and echo please the expert ear. But there is also a need for translation, literal or free, in verse or prose. The Italian saying *traduttore traditore* (translator traitor) is only a small part of the truth. A translation can open a window on a new world, as Chapman's Homer did for Keats. It can also open a door to the original, as Peter Hadley suggests in his Introduction.

Verse-to-verse translation is fiendishly difficult. Classical prosody had a quantitative base which is alien to English poetry, so not only does the translator have to convey the literal meaning: he must also find a modern verse-form which approximates to the weight and tone of the classical one. Many translators put so much effort into achieving these two things that they lose the bite and immediacy of the original. It is one of Peter Hadley's virtues that he generally gets the point of the poem across so clearly. A good example is his rendering of the last lines of Horace's *Ode to Pyrrha*. This has been a famous test-piece for translators from Milton onwards, yet few if any have conveyed the metaphor of the votive offering to Neptune as successfully as he does.

Peter Hadley is a classical scholar who chose a business career, and I have followed the same path. We both have connections with

Bristol University, and Bristol Classical Press is publishing this book. These would have been reasons enough for me to write this Foreword. That I feel honoured to do so is due to the exceptional felicity of his translations. I am delighted that this book will give them a wider readership.

Jeremy Morse

Opening the Door

Ever since my schooldays the translation of poetry has confronted me with a challenge difficult to resist. It began with the rendering of English verse into Latin elegiacs or Greek iambics, but this was no more than a mental exercise, indulged in under compulsion and producing a purely personal satisfaction. Then came the reverse process of translating classical poetry into its English equivalent, a task both more difficult and more rewarding. More difficult, because the translator has the dual problem of producing English versions that are scholastically accurate yet poetically readable. More rewarding, because if he succeeds he can enable others to enjoy literature which would otherwise remain, literally, a closed book.

My own translations of classical poetry have hitherto been shared only with a few friends, whose encouragement now prompts me to offer them to a wider public. Year by year, the study of Greek and Latin in our schools and universities continues to decline, threatening a time when the so-called dead languages will become really and truly dead, and the poets of Greece and Rome will be consigned to oblivion. Hence my compulsive desire to open up this treasure-store to others, who can at least enjoy some of its contents in translation even if they cannot read the originals. I hope that these translations may also find favour with fellow classicists, to whose critical judgment I submit them with all due deference.

I must emphasise that this does not pretend to be a comprehensive volume of classical translations, such as those already available elsewhere, but is merely a selective anthology of verses which happen to appeal to me, and which I hope others may also enjoy. The sheer size of some existing publications can be off-putting to the layman, who might prefer a more digestible intro-duction to the pleasures of classical verse. Moreover, too many existing translations, while conveying well enough the *sense* of the text, fail lamentably to capture the *spirit* of the originals in readable poetic English. At a time when traditional poetic values have been largely discarded in favour of more prosaic verse forms, I have preferred to retain metre and rhyme, believing them essential for conveying in English the charm, or wit, of the verses translated. The Greek and Latin epigrams, in particular, use elegiac couplets to express simple ideas in the most concise way. As J.W. Mackail put it, it is a metre 'equally suited to the epitaph of a hero or the verses accompanying a birthday present, a light jest or a great moral idea, the sigh of a lover or the lament over a perished empire'. Even though rhyme plays no part in classical verse, the best way of rendering these polished gems into English is, I believe, to use rhyming couplets or quatrains. To dispense with any rigid verse form, as so many modern translators have done, not only produces pedestrian results, but makes it so much easier to write what passes for poetry that the problem of translation ceases to offer the same intellectual challenge.

The hexameters of Homer and Lucretius require a rather freer English poetic form. The hexameter, despite the valiant efforts of C.S. Calverley and others, does not lend itself to the natural rhythm and intonation of English, while heroic couplets become monotonous in excess. I have therefore chosen blank verse as the most suitable medium for translating these longer poems, apart from one Lucretian passage where I have experimented with rhyme.

While accurate translation has been my goal, I have occasionally permitted myself a freer interpretation of the original text for the sake of readability. My translation of Martial's *Man About Town* is an extreme example: elsewhere I have sometimes merely omitted a few words not essential in conveying the poet's meaning.

In these verses the thoughts and emotions of poets long departed live on for us, awakening in our hearts the same echo that Flecker so confidently transmitted to the poets of the future –

> I who am dead a thousand years
>   And wrote this sweet archaic song,
> Send you my words for messengers
>   The way I shall not pass along.
>
> Since I can never see your face,
>   And never shake you by the hand,
> I send my soul through time and space
>   To greet you. You will understand.

On library shelves and in second-hand bookshops these treasures lie awaiting discovery, enshrined in language which to each successive generation is, unhappily, less and less intelligible. I shall never cease to be grateful to those who opened the door to them for me. I should like to think that in my turn I may have opened it, just a little way, for others.

Peter Hadley

FROM THE GREEK

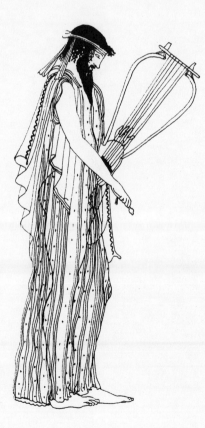

Homer

Controversy has raged over the shadowy figure of Homer, the earliest Greek poet whose work has come down to us. Even the ascription to him of the two great poems, the *Iliad* and the *Odyssey*, has been questioned, while some credit him only with the former. We need not concern ourselves here with such scholastic argument, content simply to enjoy these wonderful poems, astonishingly transmitted from the dark ages by word of mouth until put into written form during the sixth century BC, when they came to be recited at the Panathenaic festival in Athens.

The date and place of Homer's birth are equally uncertain. Linguistic evidence suggests that he came from Ionia in Asia Minor, where the Greeks had established themselves from early times. The historian Herodotus, himself a native of Ionia, tells us that Homer lived not more than four hundred years before his own time, i.e. about 830 BC. If so, Homer's accounts of the Trojan War and its sequel were probably composed some four hundred years after the events they purport to describe.

Although some scholars have even questioned whether the Trojan War ever took place, there can surely be little doubt that it did. Homer naturally used poetic licence in embroidering his account with mythological references, and indeed it is these that lend the poems much of their unique charm. Whether the abduction of Helen by the Trojan prince Paris was the real or sole cause of the war may well be doubted. It seems more likely, as has been suggested, that what prompted the Greeks to military action was that the Trojans, taking advantage of their situation commanding the narrow straits of the Dardanelles, were levying duties on Greek trade with their colonies in the Black Sea, or otherwise interrupting communications.

1

ACHILLES AND THETIS

It is the tenth year of the Trojan War (believed to have been about 1200 BC), and the Greek (Achaean) army continues to meet resistance. A priest of Apollo, Chryses, comes to their camp and asks them to release his daughter, Chryseis, whom King Agamemnon is holding captive. He offers a generous ransom, but Agamemnon brusquely refuses his request, whereupon Chryses prays to Apollo to avenge him. Apollo answers by inflicting a plague on the Greeks, which decimates their ranks.

After nine disastrous days, the Greeks hold an assembly. Achilles urges Agamemnon to consult a seer, to learn why Apollo is angry. Calchas the prophet says that the plague will not end till they release Chryseis. Agamemnon says he will only give up the girl if Achilles lets him have his own prize, Briseis, to replace her. Achilles is forced to agree, but vows he will take no further part in the fighting till the wrong done to him is righted. The time will come, he says, when they will sorely need him.

Achilles goes to the seashore and prays to his mother, Thetis, the sea goddess, for help. He asks her to go to Olympus, home of the gods, and persuade Zeus to side with the Trojans, so that the Greeks may be driven back and made to realise how much they have need of him. They will then have to atone for their treatment of him before he will consent to join the fight again.

Meanwhile a ship commanded by Odysseus is sent to Chryse (home of Chryses) to return Chryseis and make a sacrifice to propitiate Apollo.

Achilles and Thetis

> Then Thetis, weeping, answered, 'Ah, my son,
> Why did I bring you forth and nurture you
> For such unhappiness? If only you
> Could have remained in safety by your ships,
> Untouched by grief, since Fate for you decrees
> So short a life! Alas, how sad it is
> That you of all mankind must die so young,
> And how ill-starred the day I gave you birth!
> To snow-capped Mount Olympus I will go,

To Zeus the lord of thunder, and I hope
My tale will move him. As for you, remain
Here by your speedy ships in anger still
At the Achaeans, joining not at all
In any fighting. Only yesterday
Zeus went to Oceanus, to attend
A banquet with the worthy Ethiopes,
And with him too went all the other gods.
Twelve days from now he will be back again:
Then to his brazen palace I will go
To clasp his knees in supplication, nor
Will he, I think, be deaf to my appeal.'

Thus spake the goddess, and departed thence,
Leaving him sick at heart for having lost
His girdled paramour, of whom perforce
He had been dispossessed. Odysseus then
Arrived at Chryse with the sacrifice
He was to offer, and when they were safe
In the deep harbour there, they lowered sail
And in the black ship stowed it all away,
Let down the forestays, neatly dropped the mast,
And brought her to her mooring under oars.
Then out they threw the stones to anchor her,
Made fast the ropes astern, leapt out themselves
Upon the beach, whereon they disembarked
The oxen for Apollo's sacrifice,
And lastly from their ocean-going craft
Stepped Chryseis. Then that wise counsellor
Odysseus to the altar led her, and
Restored her to the father whom she loved.
'Chryses,' said he, 'King Agamemnon sent
Me here to bring your daughter back to you
And offer up a holy sacrifice
To Phoebus from the Danaans, to appease
The wrath of him who now inflicts on them
Such grievous troubles.' Saying which, he gave
The girl into his hands, and he received
With joy his darling daughter. Next they placed
The sacred offerings in readiness

3

Around the well-built altar, washed their hands
And then took up the sacrificial grains.
Then Chryses, arms uplifted, spoke this prayer:
'Thou of the silver bow, protector god
Of Chryse, Lord of Tenedos, didst hear
That other prayer of thy petitioner,
And struck the Achaean host a mighty blow:
Now therefore grant my wish a second time
And save them from disaster.' Thus he prayed,
And Phoebus heard him.

When the sun went down
And darkness came, they all lay down to sleep
Beside the stern ropes. But as soon as dawn
With rosy fingers lit the eastern sky,
They woke and made all ready to rejoin
The great Achaean army, stepped the mast
And hauled the white sails up. The archer god
Apollo sent a favourable wind
Which filled the canvas, and a gleaming wave
Gurgled around the onward-thrusting keel
Cleaving its ocean path. And when they reached
The great Achaean camp, they leapt ashore,
Hauled their black vessel high upon the strand
And fixed the tall props under her, which done
To huts and ships they went their several ways.

Meanwhile the son of Peleus, goddess-born
Achilles fleet of foot, still sat and nursed
His wrath beside his ocean-going ships,
Taking no part in councils of the great,
Nor in the war, but eating out his heart
With inactivity, and longing for
The din of battle. When the twelfth day dawned,
The immortal gods, with Zeus to lead the way,
Returned to Mount Olympus, all of them,
And Thetis, mindful of her son's appeal,
Rose from the depths of ocean heavenward
And up to great Olympus. There she found
The all-seeing son of Kronos set apart

4

From all the others on Olympus's
Most lofty peak, and sitting at his side
She put one suppliant hand upon his knees,
While with the other underneath his chin
She thus implored the ruler of the gods:
'O Zeus, our Father, if in time gone by
I ever served thee well by word or deed,
Grant this my plea, look kindly on my son,
Already destined to an early death,
Whom now King Agamemnon hath abused
In taking from him Briseis, his prize.
Lord of Olympus, Zeus all-wise, avenge
My son, and let the tide of battle flow
Against the Achaeans, till they shall atone
For their offence, and pay him due respect.'

Thus Thetis spake. Yet Zeus who drives the clouds
Made no reply, but sat in silence. She
Still held his knees and clung to him, and then
Appealed to him again: 'Now either make
A solemn pledge to me, and nod your head,
Or else, as is your right, reject my plea
And I shall know beyond a doubt that I,
Of all the gods, am least in your esteem.'
Then answered Zeus, the driver of the clouds,
Much troubled: 'What a grievous thing is this
You ask of me, that cannot fail to rouse
The wrath of Hera, who is sure to hurl
Reproachful words at me. Why, even now
She keeps on nagging me in front of all
The immortal gods because, she says, I help
The Trojans in the war. But leave me now
Lest she suspects, and I will cogitate
How best I can accomplish what you ask.
But first, to satisfy you, I will nod
My head, for this among the immortal gods
Is recognised to be the surest sign
Of my intent, and when I nod, there's no
Way round, no false excuse, no turning back.'
At which the son of Kronos gave a nod

5

Of his dark brows, and from his head divine
The immortal locks fell forward, and the whole
Of vast Olympus trembled at the sign.

And so, their conversation at an end,
They parted, she into the ocean depths
From glittering Olympus, Zeus unto
His palace, and the gods together rose
To greet their Father's entry from their seats,
For there was none that dared, when he appeared,
To sit, but all stood up to honour him.
Then sat he on his throne, but Hera knew
Full well that Thetis of the silver feet,
The daughter of the Old Man of the Sea,
Had hatched a plot with him, and straight away
She let her lord, the son of Kronos, have
The sharp edge of her tongue. 'Which of the gods,
You artful wretch, have you now once again
Been scheming with? There's nothing you like more
Than, when my back is turned, to settle things
In some deceitful way: you never dare
To tell me frankly what you have in mind.'
To whom the father of all gods and men
Made answer thus: 'Now, Hera, don't expect
That you are ever going to be aware
Of all I say, for even though you are
My consort, you would find the knowledge hard.
Whatever it is right for you to hear,
That you shall be the first of gods and men
To learn: but when I choose to make my plans
Upon my own, without the other gods,
You must not question me or seek to learn
About such things.' Then ox-faced Hera spoke
In answer: 'Son of Kronos, most revered,
What's this you're saying? Verily, till now
Never have I once questioned you or sought
To learn your plans, but I have been content
To leave you undisturbed to work your will.
But now I have a strong presentiment
That Thetis, goddess of the silver feet,

6

The daughter of the Old Man of the Sea,
May win you over to some scheme of hers,
For earlier today she sat with you
And clasped your knees, which gives me cause to think
You have agreed to drive the Achaeans back
Towards their ships, and there to slaughter them
And so avenge Achilles.' Then spake Zeus,
The driver of the clouds, and answered her:
'My lady, always you keep wondering,
And nothing that I do goes unobserved:
But there is not a thing that you can do,
Except to rouse my anger even more,
Which will be all the worse for you. If things
Are as you say they are, you may be sure
It is my pleasure that it should be so.
Come, sit in silence and obey my word,
Or all the Olympian gods will not avail
To come to your assistance, when I lay
Upon you my unconquerable hands.'

Now when his ox-faced queen heard Zeus's words
She was afraid, and sat there daring not
To answer him, but governing her heart:
And daunted too were all the other gods
In Zeus's palace. Then Hephaestus spoke,
The great artificer, anxious to help
His mother, white-armed Hera, whom he loved:
'It will be grievous and intolerable
Indeed if both of you should quarrel thus
About mere mortals, starting arguments
Among the gods. Besides, we can't enjoy
Our splendid banquet, when such paltry things
Preoccupy us. So let me advise
My mother, who well knows the sense of it,
To mollify my dearest father, Zeus,
Lest he again upbraid her and disturb
Our dinner. For, if it should be his will,
The Olympian lord of lightning, he can blast
Us from our seats, because he is so much
More powerful than all of us. So now

7

Placate his wrath with honeyed words, and then
The Olympian will be kind to us again.'
Whereat he took a double-handled cup
And gave it to his mother with these words:
'Have patience, Mother, troubled though you are,
And keep your temper, lest I have to see
You that I love chastised before my eyes,
And I shall not, however much distressed,
Have power to help you, for the Olympian's might
Brooks no resistance. Once, when I made bold
To take your side, he grabbed me by the foot
And hurled me earthwards out of Heaven's gate.
All day I fell, and at the sunset hour
Landed on Lemnos, very nearly dead,
Whereon the Sintians looked after me.'

Hera, the white-armed goddess, smiled at this,
And smiling still she took from him the cup.
And then, from left to right in turn, he poured
The nectar sweet for all the other gods
Out of the jug, and they, the blessed ones,
Could not repress their laughter as they watched
Hephaestus bustling up and down the hall.
And so with hearty appetite they dined
All day till sunset, share and share alike,
With music from Apollo's tuneful lyre
And from the Muses rounds of lovely song.
Then, when the sun's bright lantern left the sky,
They all went home to bed, each to his house
That lame Hephaestus, famed artificer,
Had built so skilfully. And homeward then
To bed went also Zeus the Olympian,
Lord of the lightning, up the stairs to where,
Whenever slumber sweetly came to him,
He always lay, and here he went to sleep:
Beside him, Hera of the golden throne.

Iliad I, 413-611

HECTOR AND ANDROMACHE

The Trojan War is being fiercely contested, with fluctuating fortunes and much slaughter. When the Trojans are hard pressed, with the Greek army at the city walls, King Priam's son Hector, the nation's hero, prepares to sally forth and lead a counter-attack. Hector's wife, Andromache, alarmed by reports of the fighting, climbs the tower to pray for help to the goddess Athene, and see for herself what is happening. Here Hector finds her in much distress, with their infant son, Astyanax, and Homer gives us this moving account of their meeting.

Sadly, Andromache's forebodings were destined to be realised, for although the Greeks were repulsed and driven back to their ships, they were eventually victorious. Hector was slain by Achilles, and – thanks to the stratagem of the Trojan horse – Troy was taken and sacked. In the division of the prisoners Andromache fell to Neoptolemus, and was carried off to Epirus in northern Greece, where she bore him three sons. Astyanax did not survive the capture of the city.

Hector and Andromache

> Then home came Hector of the shining helm
> But found not there white-armed Andromache,
> Who on the rampart with her little child
> And long-robed maid was crying out her heart.
> Finding his noble consort not within
> He stood upon the threshold, and addressed
> The servant girls. 'Come, girls, and tell me true:
> White-armed Andromache, where has she gone
> Away from home? To visit those who are
> Her kin by marriage, or to Athene's shrine
> Where other fair-tressed Trojan women go
> To ask the mighty goddess for her help?'
> Then spake a busy housemaid in reply:
> 'Since, Hector, you have asked us for the truth,
> To no such places has your lady gone,
> But up to Troy's great rampart, having heard
> That 'neath the onslaught of the Achaean host

9

The Trojans were hard-pressed; and so in haste,
Like a mad thing, she ran to climb the wall,
The nurse beside her carrying the babe.'
Thus spoke the housemaid, and immediately
Hector rushed out and made his way again
Through the great town, along the builded streets,
Until he came unto the Skaian gate
Whence he would issue out upon the plain.
Here came Andromache, his dowered wife,
Running to meet him, daughter of the great
Eëtion, who used to dwell in Thebes
Below the woods of Plakos, where he was
Cilician king: it was his daughter that
The brazen-armoured Hector had to wife.

So then she met him, having at her side
Her handmaid with the infant in her arms,
A helpless babe, the darling of his heart,
The little Hector, like a lovely star,
Whom Hector called Skamandrios, but named
By other men Astyanax, because
Prince Hector was the shield of Ilium.
Seeing the child, he gave a quiet smile,
But standing at his side Andromache
Could not restrain her tears. She took his hand
In hers, and pleaded passionately thus:
'My lord,' she sobbed, 'do you not see your strength
Will ruin you? Have you no pity then
For us – your baby son and hapless wife,
Too soon your widow? For the Achaean host
Will soon attack and slay you, and for me
If I should lose you, death were better far
With none to give me comfort in my loss.
Bereft of parents I: Eëtion,
My father, by Achilles done to death
When he laid waste the great Cilician town,
Thebes of the lofty gates; but though he slew
Eëtion my father, he forbore
To strip his corpse, but placed it on the pyre
With all its panoply, and raised above

A mound to mark the spot. The mountain nymphs,
Daughters of Zeus that bears the mighty shield,
Caused elms to grow about his resting place.
And in my house were seven brothers too.
All sent to Hades on the selfsame day
And all by swift Achilles slain, among
The shambling oxen and the woolly sheep.
My mother, once of wooded Plakos queen,
He carried off with all his other spoil,
But for a countless ransom sent her home,
Where in her father's dwelling Artemis,
The archer goddess, came and struck her down.
All these are dead and gone. So, Hector, you
Are father, mother, brother, husband mine!
Have pity on me! Stay upon these walls
And do not leave your baby fatherless,
Your wife a widow. Place a troop on guard
By yonder fig-tree, where the town's defence
Is weakest and the wall surmountable:
Thrice have the noblest of the enemy,
The princes Ajax both, and the renowned
Idomeneus, come hither to attack,
Likewise the sons of Atreus, and the brave
Offspring of Tydeus – all at this same spot.
Either some oracle has shown the way
Or else their own stout hearts have led them on.'

Then Hector of the shining helm replied,
'My lady wife, to this will I attend,
But great my shame before the men of Troy
And Trojan women of the trailing robe
If I should, like a coward, shun the war,
Nor am I so inclined, for I was taught
Ever to be courageous and to fight
Up in the forefront of the Trojan line,
To glorify my father and myself.
This much I know for sure within my heart,
That Troy, our holy citadel, is doomed
To perish soon. King Priam shares its fate
And all his people: yet 'tis not for them

11

I grieve, for Priam, nor for Hecuba,
Nor for my princely brothers that must fall
In mortal combat reddening the dust,
But rather 'tis for you, unhappy wife,
Destined to see the far Achaean land
In sad captivity, to work the loom
In some strange house of Argos, or to serve
Some woman of Messene, or perhaps
Hyperia, constrained by circumstance
To fetch and carry water. Men will say,
Seeing your tearful face, "That woman there
Was wife of Hector, noblest prince of all
The Trojan host that fought for Ilium."
Thus will they talk, and you will find it hard
Alone to bear the bonds of slavery,
Bereft of husband. May I rather die
And may the earth be heaped above my corpse
Ere I should hear the sound of your lament
Or learn the news of your captivity.'

Thus Hector spoke, and reached a shining arm
To embrace his son, at which the little boy
Burst into tears and clutched his nurse's breast,
Affrighted by the gleaming of the bronze
His father wore, and by the hairy plume
That nodded on his helmet awesomely.
Great Hector laughed, as did Andromache,
Then, pulling off his helmet, laid it down
To kiss the boy and dandle him awhile
Before he prayed: 'O Zeus and other gods,
Grant that this son of mine may emulate
My fame among the Trojans, and become
A mighty ruler here in Ilium;
That when he journeys homeward from the wars
All men may say of him, "He hath outstripped
The glory of his father"; may he slay
His enemies and seize their armament,
That so his mother may be proud of him.'
Then Hector put the boy into the arms
Of his dear wife, who smiling through her tears

Received the infant at her fragrant breast;
On seeing which, her husband felt a pang
Of pity for her. Reaching out his hand
To stroke her arm, he said, 'My lady fair,
Let not your heart fret overmuch for me:
No man shall send me down into the pit
Before my time. I tell you, once the hand
Of fate begins to write his destiny,
Coward or hero, none can then escape
Whatever is ordained. Now go you home,
Attend to all the business of the house,
Your distaff and your loom, and tell the girls
To go about their work. As to the war,
The men of Troy will make it their concern
– None more than I.' Thus noble Hector spoke
And donned again his helmet with its plume,
While his beloved wife, Andromache,
Shedding hot tears and looking back at him
Over her shoulder, homeward made her way.

Iliad, VI, 369-496

ODYSSEUS AND NAUSICAA

In his second epic, the *Odyssey*, Homer recounts the many adventures of Odysseus on his long and frequently interrupted return voyage to his home on the island of Ithaca. Taken captive by the Cyclops Polyphemus, Odysseus escapes, only to be detained again, first for a year by the sorceress Circe (who turns his men into swine), and then for a further seven years by the nymph Calypso. At long last he nears his home, but is shipwrecked once more, this time on the island of Scheria (probably Corfu), where he falls asleep in the bushes on the shore. The island is inhabited by the Phaeacians, ruled by King Alcinous, whose charming daughter, the princess Nausicaa, is the subject of this delightful story.

Odysseus and Nausicaa

> Long-suffering Odysseus rested there
> By sleep and his exertions overcome.
> Then went Athene to the land and town
> Of the Phaeacians: they in former days
> Had dwelt in broad Hyperia, neighbours of
> The Cyclopes, a most aggressive race,
> Who used their greater strength to harry them,
> Until one day their king, Nausithous,
> A godlike man, bestirred them to migrate
> And found a new abode in Scheria,
> Far from rapacious men. And there he built
> Them houses with a city wall round,
> And temples of the gods, distributing
> A plot of land to each. But he long since
> Had gone to Hades, overcome by fate,
> And been succeeded by Alcinous,
> Divine in wisdom. 'Twas to his abode
> Owl-faced Athene now betook herself,
> Designing brave Odysseus's return.
>
> She entered there the richly furnished room
> Where slept a girl in face and form divine,
> The lovely daughter of Alcinous,

Princess Nausicaa, while close at hand
Two maids-in-waiting by the gleaming doors
Lay fair as Graces, one on either side.
Closed though they were, yet like a breath of wind
The goddess through them passed to reach the bed,
Disguised as the princess's bosom friend,
A girl of her own age, whose father was
A man called Dymas, captain of a ship.
Hers was the voice Athene now assumed
As, standing o'er Nausicaa, she said:
'Nausicaa, why did your mother bear
A child so thoughtless? See, your pretty clothes
Lie all uncared for, and yet soon enough
You will be married, and you will require
A trousseau for yourself, and must provide
For those who have to give the bride away.
A girl's good name depends upon such things,
Which also bring her parents happiness.
And so, as soon as shining dawn appears,
Let's go a-washing: I will come and help
To get it done as soon as possible,
For it will not be long before you're wed:
Already now are many noblemen
Your suitors in the land where you were born.
Come, ask your royal father to prepare,
When morning comes, a wagon and some mules,
Which we can load with girdles, robes and wraps
Of splendid hue. 'Twill be much easier
For us to travel thus than go on foot
– The washing-troughs are far away from here.'
Thus spake owl-faced Athene, and returned
To Mount Olympus, where the gods, they say,
Have their eternal home, by winds unmoved,
Untouched by rain, by snowstorms unassailed,
With radiance all around: the happy ones
Pass here their endless days in sweet content.
Here went the goddess when she left the girl.

As soon as Dawn sat on her lovely throne
She woke fair-robed Nausicaa. At once

She marvelled at her dream, and made her way
Along the palace corridors to tell
Her father and her mother, whom she found
At home, her mother sitting with her maids
Spinning sea-purple yarn upon the hearth,
Her father on the point of going out
To join a princely council, whither he
Had been invited by his noblemen.
She went up very close to him, and said:
'Oh, daddy darling, could you please arrange
To have a nice big cart with good strong wheels
Made ready for me, so that I can take
My pretty clothes, now lying dirty here,
And wash them in the river? Yours as well,
For when you go with nobles to confer
You must have freshly laundered things to wear.
Besides, you have five sons within your house,
Two of them married, but the other three
Are single yet and lead a merry life,
For ever wanting raiment newly washed
To wear at dances. All this worries me.'

Thus spake Nausicaa, for she did not like
To speak of marriage to her father dear,
But he knew well her thoughts, and answered her:
'I would not grudge you mules, my darling child,
Or anything you want. Go then, of course,
And I will ask the servants to prepare
A good strong wagon fitted with a hood.'
He called the servants, and they set to work
To bring outside a smoothly running cart
And harness up the mules, while she went off
To fetch the splendid raiment from the store
And placed it all upon the polished cart.
Meanwhile her mother filled a picnic box
With appetising food of every kind,
And little dainties, and she poured some wine
Into a goatskin bag. And when the girl
Climbed up into the cart, she handed her
A golden flask of olive oil, wherewith

16

She and her handmaids might anoint themselves.
Nausicaa took the whip and gleaming reins
And flicked the mules to send them on their way:
They, hooves a-clatter, strode out eagerly,
Pulling their freight of clothes and her as well,
While her attendants kept her company.
And when they reached the lovely river's edge,
Its washing pools unfailingly supplied
With purest water bubbling copiously,
Enough to clean the dirtiest of clothes,
They loosed the yoke and drove the mules to graze
The honeyed sward beside the swirling stream,
Then from the wagon took the clothes and dropped
Them in the murky water, where each strove
To be the first to tread them in the troughs.

When all the dirty clothes were laundered clean
They spread them out in line beside the sea,
Just where it washed the shingle on the beach.
This done, they took a bathe, and rubbed themselves
With olive oil, then on the river bank
They had their picnic, waiting for the sun
To dry the clothes. And when they had enjoyed
Their meal, the princess and her servant girls,
They all took off their hats, and played a game
Of ball, while she, white-armed Nausicaa,
Led off the singing. As when Artemis,
The archer-goddess, goes along the peaks
Of Erymanthus or Taÿgetus
To hunt the wild boar or the nimble deer,
The nymphs, all daughters of almighty Zeus,
Join in the sport, and gladden Leto's heart,
Yet Artemis in face and form outstrips
Them all, and though they all are beautiful,
Stands out among them, so among her maids
The virgin princess was conspicuous.

But when at last the time for her return
Was almost come, and she had yoked the mules
And folded up the fine apparel, then

17

Athene caused Odysseus to awake
And see the lovely girl who was to guide
Him into the Phaeacian capital.
So when the princess made to throw the ball
To one of her attendant girls, she missed
The girl she aimed at, and it fell instead
Into a deep rock pool, whereat they gave
A piercing shriek, at which Odysseus woke,
And sitting up he pondered in his heart:
'Alas! To what strange land have I now come,
What kind of people? Lawless savages,
Or hospitable men who fear the gods?
Methought I heard just now the cry of girls
– Of nymphs, perhaps, who on the mountain tops
Or in the streams and meadows have their home,
Or am I near to folk of human tongue?
Come, I'll explore and find out for myself.'
Thus spake godlike Odysseus, and rose up
From his concealment in the undergrowth.
With stout right hand he broke from off a tree
A leafy branch to hide his nakedness,
And sallied forth, just like a mountain lion
Who, trusting in his strength, through wind and rain
With eyes ablaze goes out to hunt the ox,
Sheep or wild deer, by hunger even forced
To raid the pens within the homestead walls;
So, naked though he was, Odysseus dared
Approach the fair-tressed maidens in his woe.
Besmeared with brine, he was a fearsome sight
And sent them running helter-skelter up
The sandy beach. One only stood her ground,
The daughter of Alcinous, in whom
Athene planted courage, and deterred
Her trembling legs from joining in the flight.

Odysseus pondered whether he should throw
His arms around the lovely maiden's knees
And so entreat her, or from some way off
Use honeyed words to make his plea to her
That she should guide his footsteps to the town

And give him clothing. But he thought it best
To keep his distance and rely on speech,
Lest if he clasped her knees she took offence,
So spake he gentle and well-chosen words:
'I beg you, tell me, miss, are you a god
Or mortal creature? If a god you be,
One dwelling in the broad expanse of heaven,
I reckon from your face and form and height
You must be Artemis, the daughter of
Almighty Zeus: but if you mortal be
And dwell on earth, thrice blest must be your sire,
Thrice blest your mother and your brothers too.
What heartfelt happiness they must enjoy
To see a girl like you begin the dance!
But happiest of all will be the man
Who wins you for his own with wedding gifts
And brings you to his home, for never yet
Have I beheld such beauty here on earth
In man or woman. Looking at you now
I needs must worship, just as I revered
A little palm I saw in Delos once,
Close by Apollo's altar growing up.
I went there as the leader of a host
And little knew the troubles then in store
Upon that expedition. There I stood
And marvelled at the little tree, than which
No lovelier sapling ever sprang from earth.
Just so I marvel now on seeing you,
My lady, and with such a sense of awe
I dare not clasp your knees, for all my woe.
'Twas only yesterday that I escaped
The wine-dark sea, on which for twenty days,
Leaving the island of Ogygia,
I suffered all the fury of the storm.
But now some god has cast me on this shore,
Perhaps to suffer more disasters here:
I dare not think that they are at an end,
But only that the gods have plenty still
In store for me. Be merciful, my queen,
For after all my many sufferings

19

You are the first I come to, knowing none
Of those who live here. Guide me to the town,
Give me some rags to clothe my nakedness,
If only what you wrapped your linen in
When here you came. And in return I pray
The gods may grant you all your heart's desire,
Husband and home, peace and prosperity,
For there is nothing better than when man
And wife can live in mental harmony,
Confounding enemies, delighting friends,
But knowing best themselves their happiness.'

Then answered him white-armed Nausicaa:
'You seem no rascal, stranger, and no fool:
Olympian Zeus it is who at his whim
Dispenses happiness to mortal men,
To good and bad alike, as he may choose.
'Tis he that brought on you these miseries,
And you must suffer them as best you can.
Since now to this our country you have come,
And to our city, you shall not go short
Of clothes, nor yet of any other thing
Which after so much suffering you might
Come begging for. I'll guide you to the town
And tell you who lives here. This is the land
Of the Phaeacians, this their city: I
Am daughter of Alcinous, the king
From whom they draw their strength and livelihood.'
Thus spake Nausicaa, and shouted out
To her fair-tressed attendants, 'Girls, come here!
Wherever are you running, just because
You've seen a man? You surely do not think
He comes to us in enmity? Not he
Nor any man yet born have ever come
In arms against our land: we are too dear
To the immortal gods for this to be.
Here far, far off upon the rolling sea
We have our home, and no one else on earth
Comes near us. But this hapless wanderer
Has reached our shores, and we must succour him,

For Zeus is ever well disposed towards
Strangers and beggars, and however small
The gift, he loves the giver. Come then, girls,
And give the stranger food and drink, and wash
Him in the river, sheltered from the wind.'
On hearing her reproof, they checked their flight,
Calling to one another, and then came
And showed Odysseus where he could sit down
Out of the wind, just as Nausicaa
Had told them, daughter of Alcinous.
Next, they set down a tunic and a cloak
Beside him, then they brought a golden flask
Of olive oil, and bade him take a bath
Within the rushing stream. But he demurred
And thus made answer to the servant girls:
'Girls, stay there at a distance, if you please,
That I myself may wash the salty brine
From off my shoulders, and anoint myself
With olive oil, which I have lacked so long.
I cannot wash myself in front of you,
For I'm ashamed to stand here in the nude
Among you fair-tressed girls.' And so they went
Away and told Nausicaa what he'd said.

Then in the stream Odysseus washed his back
And big broad shoulders of the barren salt,
Likewise his head, encrusted all with brine,
And then when he was clean he rubbed himself
With oil. and donned the clothes the young princess
Had given him. And Zeus's daughter now,
Athene, made him look still sturdier
And taller, and she caused his hair to grow
As thick as hyacinth upon his head.
As when Hephaestus and Athene both
Have taught a skilful craftsman how to put
A lovely finish on some work of art
By pouring gold on silver, so she now
Gave head and shoulders both an added touch.
Then went Odysseus off a little way
And sat upon the seashore, radiant

With grace and beauty. Whereupon the girl
Admiringly regarded him, and said
To her fair-tressed attendants: 'Listen now,
My white-armed maids, there's something I must say.
'Tis not without the knowledge of the gods
Who dwell on Mount Olympus that this man
Joins the Phaeacians, near to gods themselves.
He seemed before to have a sorry look,
But now he looks exactly like the gods
Whose home is in the broad expanse of heaven.
I wish that such a man might live with us
And be my husband. How I hope he may
Decide to stay here! But come on now, girls,
And let the stranger have some food and drink.'
Thus spake she, and they heeded her command
And brought Odysseus things to eat and drink,
Which he, who had such suffering endured,
Took with avidity, for it was long
Since he had had a taste of any food.

But now white-armed Nausicaa bethought
Herself of other things. She folded first
The clothes and put them on the splendid cart,
Then yoked the strong-hoofed mules, and climbing up,
Called out to tell Odysseus what to do:
'Come, stranger, now, it's time to go to town,
That I may guide you to my father's house,
Where you will meet the country's noblemen.
You seem to me to be a man of sense:
This, then, is what you have to do. As long
As we are travelling in the countryside
Among the farms, then briskly follow on
Behind the mule-cart with my servant girls,
And I will lead the way. But when we come
Close to the lofty ramparts of the town,
We'll change the plan. A splendid harbour lies
On either side our city, with between
A narrow causeway, where the rounded ships
Are beached upon the road, and each one has
Its special place. There close at hand the square,

22

Around Poseidon's lovely temple built
Of blocks of stone deep-buried in the ground.
There too they make the gear for the black ships,
Cables and ropes, and taper off the oars.
For the Phaeacians take no interest
In bow and quiver – only masts and oars
And nicely balanced ships in which they love
To go a-sailing on the grizzled sea.
'Tis my good name with them I seek to guard:
I want no tongues to gossip as I pass.
The common folk can be so insolent,
And I can guess how, after seeing us,
Some vulgar chap will say, 'Why, who is this
Tall handsome stranger with Nausicaa?
Where did she pick him up? No doubt she's found
A castaway from some far distant land,
For none lives near to us. Or else some god
Has come from heaven in answer to our prayers
To have and hold her. It is better thus
That she should find a husband for herself
From foreign parts, she thinks so little of
Phaeacians here, where many noblemen
Court her in vain.' That's how they'll talk, and I
Would suffer shame thereat. I too would blame
A girl who acted thus and went with men
Against her parents' wish before she wed.

'So, stranger, heed my words if you desire
My father to despatch you homeward bound
As soon as possible. Beside the track
You'll see a grove of poplars, sacred to
Athene, with a flowing spring in it
And meadows all around. My father there
Owns a luxuriant garden and a park
In hailing distance of the city. Sit
And wait awhile there till we get to town
And reach my father's house. When you suppose
We have arrived, go into town yourself
And make inquiry for the palace of
My father, King Alcinous. It's not hard

To recognise, and any little child
Could point it out to you, because the house
Is quite unlike all others in the land.
Now when you reach the palace and its yard,
Then swiftly cross the hall, until you come
To where my mother sits before the fire
Upon the hearth, and spins sea-purple yarn,
Her back against a pillar, with her maids
Behind her – 'tis a very pretty sight.
My father's throne is near her, where he sits
And drinks his cup of wine just like a god.
Go past him, though, and clasp my mother's knees
If you desire to celebrate, and soon,
A happy homecoming, however far
You now may be: for if you once can win
Her sympathy, then you may hope to see
Your loved ones and your fatherland again.

So said she, and applied the gleaming whip
To start the mules, which left the river bank
And stepped out briskly. But Nausicaa
Reined them well in, that they might not outpace
Odysseus and the maids, who walked behind,
And so she used discretion with the whip.
The sun was setting when at last they reached
Athene's sacred grove, renowned of men,
Where sat Odysseus down and made a prayer
To mighty Zeus's daughter: 'Hearken now,
Thou tireless child of aegis-bearing Zeus,
And grant me what I ask now, even though
Thou didst not heed my last entreaty, when
The great Poseidon, shaker of the world,
Made to destroy me. Grant that I may find
A welcome friendly and compassionate
From the Phaeacians.' Thus Odysseus prayed.
Athene heard, but stayed invisible,
Fearing her uncle, whose unwearied wrath
Against godlike Odysseus never ceased
Until the day he reached his native land.

Odyssey VI, 1-331

ODYSSEUS AND HIS DOG

Alcinous, king of the Phaeacians, welcomes the long-suffering Odysseus and provides him with a ship to carry him from Scheria on the last stage of his long journey home to Ithaca. Here he lands and is met by the swineherd Eumaeus, who, having long since given up hope of his master's survival, fails to recognise him after his twenty-years' absence. He bewails the disgraceful conduct of the suitors who have been pestering Odysseus's wife, Penelope, for her hand in marriage. Eumaeus accompanies the disguised Odysseus to his palace, where at first only his old dog, Argos, is able to identify him. This passage vividly describes the touching scene of their reunion.

Odysseus and his Dog

Such were the words they spoke among themselves:
But the dog Argos who was lying there
Lifted his head and pricked his ears; he had
Been reared by brave Odysseus, who had left
For Troy ere he could use him for the hunt.
In former times the young men took him out
With them to chase wild goats, roedeer or hares,
But now he lay uncared for, masterless,
On a great pile of dung outside the gates
Where they heaped up the droppings of the mules
And oxen, till the serfs of the estate
Carted it off to spread upon the fields.
There Argos lay, his coat a mass of fleas,
But when he saw Odysseus close to him
He wagged his tail and lowered both his ears,
Yet could no longer find sufficient strength
To join his master, who with sidelong glance
Observed him there, and wiped away a tear
Which he contrived Eumaeus should not see.
'Eumaeus,' said Odysseus hastily,
'How very strange it is that they allow
This dog to lie here on a heap of dung
– A splendid beast, although I cannot know
If he has speed to match his fine physique,

Or if he's just a house-dog, such as those
Mere vanity will prompt a man to keep.'
To which the swineherd gave him this reply:
'That was a man indeed to whom this dog
Belonged, who perished far away from home:
If he still had the powers that were his
When Lord Odysseus left to go to Troy,
You'd be amazed to see his speed and strength.
No beast of prey that ever he pursued
Escaped the chase: however dense the wood
He tracked them down, but now he is reduced
To such a state of misery as this,
His master dead in some far foreign land,
Uncared for by the palace servant girls.
When master is not there to supervise,
You may be sure that servants misbehave,
And once a man is brought to slavery
He is but half the man he was before.'
Whereat Eumaeus went inside the house
And found the suitor nobles gathered there
Within the hall. But suddenly, just when
He'd seen his master after twenty years,
Black death claimed faithful Argos for his own.

Odyssey XVII, 290-327

26

Anacreon

Anacreon was an Ionian lyric poet who flourished about 530 BC. Despite a life of dissolute living, he survived to the age of eighty-three, eventually dying by choking on a grape stone. Some scholars have questioned the attribution of this and other poems to Anacreon himself, and believe them to be later imitations of his work, to be classified as Anacreontea.

Cicada

O Cicada, how we bless you
As you sit there chirruping,
Sipping dewdrops to refresh you
In the treetops, like a king.
Over everything in view
In the fields around you reign,
All the woods acknowledge you
Emperor of your domain.
Mortal men and Muses love you,
Harbinger of summer days,
And the Sun himself above you
First inspired your roundelays.
Earthborn, age can touch you never:
Songster passion-free and wise,
You deserve to live for ever
With the gods in paradise.

27

The Greek Anthology

Early in the first century before Christ, the poet Meleager collected a number of old Greek poems under the title 'The Garland', to which he himself wrote an introduction in verse. This in turn became the nucleus of later and larger collections which form the Greek Anthology as we know it today, and which contains poems written over a period of some fifteen hundred years, from about 600 BC to AD 900.

The poems in the Greek Anthology are for the most part very brief, many of them consisting of a single couplet or quatrain, and for this reason they are sometimes described as epigrams. Their subject-matter is diverse, ranging from lamentations about love or death to satirical comments on people and things. I have tried to make a representative selection, arranged so as to present the serious poems first and the more light-hearted ones later. But, of course, these are only a fraction of the whole.

The following are the approximate dates when the poets here represented were in their prime:

Simonides	500 BC	Marcus Argentarius	AD 40
Plato	380 BC	Lucilius	AD 60
Asclepiades	290 BC	Nicarchus	AD 60
Diotimus	270 BC	Strato	AD 125
Callimachus	260 BC	Lucian	AD 170
Eratosthenes	240 BC	Alpheus	AD 170
Theodorides	230 BC	Paulus Silentiarius	AD 550
Dioscorides	180 BC	Agathias	AD 550
Meleager	95 BC	Rufinus	AD 550
Philodemus	60 BC	Macedonius	AD 550

The sources of the poems translated are given in the table of Contents. Numbers in brackets refer to the Palatine Anthology, compiled by Constantine Cephalas in the tenth century AD, unless otherwise stated. P.A. denotes the Planudean Anthology compiled by Maximus Planudes in the twelfth or thirteenth century, and E.G. denotes Kaibel's Epigrammata Graeca.

In reading these poets of another age, some of whom lived more than two thousand years ago, one is struck by the close resemblance between their emotions and our own. Love, laughter, grief, compassion – all these they experienced no less than we do, and all are to be found in their poetry. Human nature has changed little through the centuries.

Liebestraum

> When Moeris said goodnight she seemed to hold me
> And kiss my lips – and yet, for all I know,
> I dreamed it. I remember all she told me
> And all I said to her, but I can show
> It was a dream: for, if the kiss was given,
> Why now am I on earth, and not in Heaven?

Strato

No Autumn

> When lovers never have to part
> Young beauty grows no older:
> Spring will not wither in the heart,
> Nor passion's flame grow colder.
>
> If she was fair but yesterday,
> Then fair she is this morning,
> And if today still fair, then pray
> Why fear tomorrow's dawning?

Strato

Rhodope

Why wash your hands, why do your hair,
Why pause your finger-nails to pare,
And why bedeck the clothes you wear
When Rhodope's no longer there?

Fair Rhodope! Unless my eyes
Can gaze on you when daylight dies,
Let them not see the golden rise
Of dawn across the eastern skies.

Paulus Silentiarius

The Winebibber

I like not wine; yet when you wish that I
Should lose my wits in it, remember this:
Sip but the cup, and I will drain it dry.
For if your lips but touch it, 'tis no bliss
Then to be sober – no, nor then deny
The sweet wine-pourer; since your tender kiss
Flies from the brim to me, and is not wasted,
But tells me of the joy the goblet tasted.

Agathias

The Rose

Too brief the rose's fragrant hour,
Too soon the bloom is dead:
If you go searching for the flower
You'll find the thorn instead.

Anon

The Suppliant

When Prodike alone I found
I hastened such a chance to seize
And put my suppliant arms around
    Her lovely knees.

' 'Tis in your power', I said, 'to save
This lover now at life's last breath:
Your choice – to rescue from the grave
    Or doom to death.'

My little darling wept to hear
What I entreating had to say,
Then gently, brushing off a tear.
    Pushed me away.

                  Rufinus

Skin Deep

'Tis little use, the lovely look
Without the grace to match it:
As with a fish, you need a hook
Behind the bait to catch it.

                  Capito

Cupid for Sale

Though clinging to his mother's breast
The infant must, yes, *must* be sold:
Why should I nurture such a pest,
Who isn't half as good as gold?

With feathered wings and scratchy nails
And little snubby nose he came:
Hear how he cackles and he wails –
Too wild for mother love to tame.

31

Restless of tongue and sharp of eye,
He can't be reared – for sale, I say!
If any merchant wants to buy
A boy, roll up, and sail away.

And yet – I wonder what to do?
My heart is softened by his yelling:
Zenophila, he'll stay with you –
Perhaps I won't insist on selling.

Meleager

Pet's Corner

Stranger, commemorated here
    'Tis but a dog you see,
And yet, I beg you, do not sneer:
    My master wept for me

– Wept as the dusty earth he pressed
    Above my lifeless head,
And wrote, where now I lie at rest,
    The words that you have read.

Anon

Love's Ally

Against Love's arrows Reason steels my heart,
In single combat he shall not defeat me:
Though mortal, I will face the immortal's dart
And suffer not his trickery to beat me.
But if great Bacchus joins him in the fray,
Against them both how can I win the day?

Rufinus

The Mosquito

Buzz off and take a telegram for me, mosquito dear;
Go, settle on the tip of my Zenophila's sweet ear:
'Are you never, never coming?' (runs the song that you'll be
    humming)
'You're forgetting how he's fretting while you're slumbering
    up here.'

Fly away and make your music – ah, but softly, if you please
(Her husband mustn't wake and hear such messages as these),
And I promise, on condition you're successful in your mission,
I'll requite you, and this night you'll be a second Hercules.

Meleager

Lonely Vigil

The lovely Niko made a vow
    That she would come to me this night.
Hour after hour I wait, but now
    She is forsworn. Put out the light.

Asclepiades

Ten to One

Ten times I toast Lysidice:
Euphrante? Once will do.
You think that L. means more to me
Than E? It isn't true.
By Bacchus, whom these lips have pressed,
Euphrante is, I swear,
Alone worth ten of all the rest,
Just as the moon up there
Outshineth, with its single light,
The starry millions of the night.

Marcus Argentarius

Prophecy

Did I not warn you, Prodike,
'Remember that we all grow old:
Decay will come and love will flee,
Alas, too soon'? This I foretold.

Now come the wrinkles and grey hairs,
The shrivelled flesh, the lips gone dry:
No ardent lovers climb your stairs,
But like a tomb we pass you by.

Rufinus

Danger Ahead

Thy summer's still in bud, thy fruit
Wears still the charm of virgin green,
Yet Cupid's bow prepares to shoot –
The fire is smouldering unseen.
Fly, all who've tasted love and sorrow:
I prophesy a blaze tomorrow.

Philodemus

Betrayal

When our pledge of love was spoken
    Softly in the darkened room,
We required no other token
    Save the lamplight and the gloom

– Gloom where now, like daylight dying.
    Love dishonoured hides his face,
While the lamplight sees you lying
    In another man's embrace.

Meleager

34

No Escape

From Heliodora, says my heart,
'Tis better far to stay apart,
Too well remembering how she
Has tortured us with jealousy.

Heart, you are right: and yet I know
I have not strength enough to go,
For she herself says 'Run away',
Then kisses me – and here I stay.

Philodemus

Love and Logic

If beauty lives but for a season,
Why then, to share it more's the reason;
But if for ever, why refuse
To give of what you cannot lose?

Strato

The Kiss

Europa's kiss can sweetness be
E'en though she only brush my lips,
Yet when Europa kisses me
She takes no gentle honey-sips,
But sucks my soul insatiably
Out of my very finger-tips.

Rufinus

Third Time Lucky?

When first of all you said me nay
Your fruit was green upon the vine;
Again, upon your vintage day,
The ripened grape would not be mine:
Do you begrudge me still – or may
I take a sip of raisin wine?

Anon

Autobiography

I came where I was not before;
I was, and now I am no more.
Should they enlarge on my career,
Mistrust them. I shall not be here.

Anon

The Reckless Lover

When to Cydilla's soft embrace I go,
By day or, bolder, at the darkling time,
I know the awful precipice I climb,
And that my life is staked upon a throw.
All this I know, and yet defy the danger:
With love to lead me, fear becomes a stranger.

Philodemus

Mycenae

How few of them are left to see,
Those citadels where long ago
The heroes lived – and those there be
By time laid low.

Hapless Mycenae, so I found
It was with thee when here I came:
More desolate than pasture ground
    Thy halls of fame.

An aged herdsman, turning down
His finger, mumbled in my ear,
'The Cyclopean treasure town,
    They say, stood here.'

Alpheus

Nicoteles

Here Philip laid to rest his son,
Nicoteles, struck down by fate:
He was but twelve, this little one
Of whom his hopes had been so great.

Callimachus

Together

How long with stolen glance and hidden fire
Must we disguise the depth of our desire?
Let's end the inner anguish, and declare
Our secret now for all the world to share,
And then, if they would heartlessly prevent
The tie that could assuage our discontent,
The sword shall be our remedy; for whether
We live or die, we're happier together.

Paulus Silentiarius

Statue of Niobe

The gods in anger turned me into stone
From flesh and blood, yet is their magic vain.
O rash Praxiteles! God's will's undone!
From stone you make me flesh and blood again.

Anon

Eyewitness

Mouth upon mouth, and breast to breast,
   Close-held I clasped Antigone.
I say no more: as to the rest,
   The lamp must testify for me.

Marcus Argentarius

Thunderstorm

Shambling unherded from the hill
Returned the oxen to their stall,
A snowy blanket on them all
   – Alas, but up there still
Long-sleeping underneath the oak
Therimachus the herdsman lies,
On whom, from out the livid skies,
   Came down the lightning stroke.

Diotimus

Starlight

Bright as the morning star you shone
Among the living; now you're gone
With equal brilliancy you shed
A sunset light among the dead.

Plato

Shipwreck

Sail on: 'twas here that Davy Jones
Became the guardian of our bones –
With dead and dying all about us
We watched them sail away without us.

Theodorides

The Bachelor

I, Dionysius, lie here dead
And Tarsus was my native city;
In sixty years I never wed:
My father did – and more's the pity.

Anon

Perjury

I swore to Aphrodite I would stay
From sweet Hedylion two whole nights away:
The goddess must have laughed, I think, because
She knew full well how much in love I was.
I cannot bear a second night apart,
So choose to break my oath, and not my heart.

Maecius

Parting

Just as I start at last to bid farewell
     I linger on and stifle my adieu,
For darker than the blackest night of Hell
     Becomes my world when I am not with you.

You are my daylight, yet you have an art
     Of sweet discourse beyond the power of day,
And all the hopes I cherish in my heart
     Are hanging on the lovely things you say.

Paulus Silentiarius

Thermopylae

Inform the Spartans we obeyed
Their orders, stranger. Here we stayed.

Simonides

Rescue

You've come to me, although I never could
In all my wildest dreams believe you would:
Now, thunderstruck, I find the dream come true,
A dream no longer, and for love of you
My heart is tossed on billows of emotion,
My soul half drowned in Aphrodite's ocean.
Behold this shipwrecked sailor, save his skin,
Lift up your harbour boom, and let him in.

Macedonius the Consul

...Three's None

I grew pale when I saw Melitë
    Today, for walking with her
Was her husband. So I said to her,
    In something of a dither,
'May I help you draw your bolt, if you
    Will graciously permit it,
And unlock the door, assuming that
    My key will chance to fit it?'
But she laughed, and with a look towards
    Her husband, answered, 'Will you
Keep away from my front door, or else
    I fear the dog may kill you!'

Eratosthenes Scholasticus

The Human Atom

The world is made, said Epicurus,
Of atoms much too small to see:
They were (he hastened to assure us)
The smallest things that there could be.
But Diophantus happened later,
Or Epicurus in his quiz
Would have pronounced the atom greater

By far than Diophantus is,
And atoms, he'd have diagnosed,
Of Diophantus are composed.

Lucilius

Pop Singer

The nightjar's grating song betokens death:
Demophilus, alas, is still alive,
And when Demophilus to sing draws breath,
Death's harbinger himself cannot survive.

Nicarchus

The Physician

When Dr Mark was looking round
The Hall of Arts, he chanced to linger;
A marble Zeus the doctor found,
And on it laid his little finger.

This was not flesh and blood, but stone;
This was a god, not mortal man:
Yet look what Dr Mark has done –
Here comes the undertaker's van!

Nicarchus

Second Voyage

The man who marries Number Two
Is like a shipwrecked sailor who,
Cast once upon some rocky shore,
Embarks again and asks for more.

Anon

Hearing the Case?

Two litigants appeared in court:
Both deaf as posts were those who fought
The case, but deafer far than they
The judge presiding on that day.

The plaintiff, being duly sworn,
Complained his neighbour ground his corn
At night: defendant's argument
Concerned five months' arrears of rent.

His Lordship looked from one to the other
And said, 'Why quarrel? She's your mother:
Towards her keep it's only fair
You each should pay an equal share.'

Nicarchus

Nightmare

A dream of Dr E. last night
    Caused Diophantus such distress
Despite the charm he clutched so tight,
    He's not recovered consciousness.

Lucilius

Gale Warning

The wind gave just a tiny puff:
Chaeremon, lighter far than fluff,
Was lifted off the ground on high
And would have hurtled through the sky,
But luckily he chanced to meet
A spider's web, and by his feet
Enmeshed hung supine in the air.
Five days and nights he stayed up there,
Then, sliding down the spider's skein,
Found *terra firma* once again.

Lucilius

Signpost to Danger

Remember, vipers must be scotched,
Laodiceans must be watched,
Likewise mad dogs – and did I mention
Laodiceans need attention?

Anon

The New Stove

Poor Heliodorus, you were sold a
Pup! That stove of yours is colder
Than the coldest wind that blows
Icy from the Thracian snows.

Stop your puffing and your poking!
Look at how the thing is smoking!
Keep your stove till summer: you'll
Find it keeps your wine so cool.

Nicarchus

S.O.S.

Saviour, Philo called his ship,
    Though if Zeus himself had braved
In the *Saviour's* hands a trip
    He could never have been saved.

When the *Saviour* slipped her berth,
    Death it was to those she bore,
Ending up on mother earth
    – Or upon the Stygian shore.

Nicarchus

43

Killed in Action

Athenion sang 'The Trojan Horse'
With such intense dramatic force
All Ilium blazed again, and I
Myself was set on fire thereby.

Unlike the Grecian host of yore
I had not fought the ten-year war,
But when the holocaust befell,
The Trojans died – and I as well.

Dioscorides

Nosey Parker

I can see a big projection that I think is Nico's nose,
And yet Nico simply isn't to be found:
Well, he can't be more than half a mile behind it, I suppose,
So he won't be very long – let's stick around.
Nico's nose goes on ahead of him: let's go up somewhere high
And then, if we are patient, we shall see him bye and bye.

Nicarchus

Star Prophet

All the astrologers declared
My uncle's life would long be spared
With quite unanimous conviction,
Save Hermocleides, whose prediction
Of early death was to his credit:
'Twas at the funeral he said it.

Lucilius

44

Gold Digger

Your name, Melissa, means a little bee:
Your name and nature perfectly agree,
For when you kiss me, on your lips is honey
– And yet you keep on stinging me for money.

Marcus Argentarius

Surgical Spirit

When Akestorides lay dead
Beneath his operating knife,
'Poor fellow,' Agelaos said,
'But he'd have had a limp for life.'

Nicarchus

Artemidora

While Artemidora was dozing
(It happens she's rather petite)
Demetrius fanned her reposing
– And blew the girl into the street.

Lucilius

Slander

Nicylla, how can they attack you
Saying that you dye your hair?
Why, I *know* that it is black – you
Bought it in the market square!

Lucilius

Brief Encounter

'Good evening, lass.' 'Good evening, Sir.' 'Now who's that just
    ahead?'
'What's that to you?' 'I'd like to know.' 'My mistress, Sir,' she
    said.
'What hope have I?' 'Of what?' 'A night.' 'Well, what have you
    to offer?'
'Some gold.' 'Aha!' 'This much...' 'No luck – too little in your
    coffer!'

Anon

Rich Man, Poor Man...

My youth was poor, today in age
    I count my money-bags,
In misery at every stage
    Of riches and of rags.
In youth I had no cash to spend
    And could have spent a lot;
Today I'm at my journey's end
    And can't spend what I've got.

Anon

Demi Pension

Asclepiades the miser in his parlour saw a mouse;
'Dear mouse,' he cried, 'what mischief are you up to in my
    house?'
Whereat the mouse laughed merrily. 'Don't worry, friend,' he
    said,
'We're not expecting breakfast. All we're asking is a bed.'

Lucilius

The Athlete

Poor Charmus, when competing with five others in a race,
Took something of a beating and obtained the seventh place.
'Impossible' – I hear you say – 'for how could he contrive
To give this pitiful display against no more than five?'
A friend of his espied him, and, although not lightly clad,
Went running on beside him, crying loudly 'Come on, lad!'
So Charmus came in seventh (as I think I said before)
– He'd have failed to be eleventh, if he'd had just five friends
    more.

Nicarchus

Vanishing Trick

A cushion Lysimachus had:
Lysimachus now hasn't got it.
Lysimachus, isn't it sad
Antiochus happened to spot it?

Lucilius

The Living Image

The portrait-painter Eutychus hath twenty sons begot
– And not a single likeness among the blooming lot!

Lucilius

Relativity

Playsafe, embarking on a spree,
Resolved that he for one would not
Get drunk. Result: he looked to be
The only drunkard of the lot.

Lucian

Bon Voyage

A sailor came one day to ask Olympicus the prophet
If he would recommend a trip to Rhodes, or put him off it.
'First, choose a brand new ship,' replied the prophet, 'and
  remember
'You must voyage in the summer, there is danger in
  December;
'You will reach your destination if you do as I advise you
' – Provided that a pirate doesn't happen to surprise you.'

Nicarchus

FROM THE LATIN

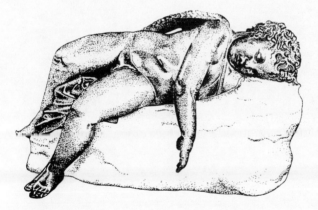

Lucretius

Lucretius (T. Lucretius Carus) was born in Rome about 94 BC and died in 55 BC. His long poem in six books, *De Rerum Natura* (*About the Nature of Things*) is an ambitious and successful attempt to expound a materialist conception of the universe in a poetic, and therefore more readable form.

Living at a time when traditional beliefs in the gods were being increasingly questioned by intellectuals, Lucretius crusaded passionately against the superstitions endemic to Roman religion. These, he considered, not only generated unnecessary phobias, but also inhibited rational philosophic thought about the nature of the universe and man's place in it. He was himself a devotee of the Epicurean philosophy, in which happiness was something to be pursued as an end in itself, and religion too often obstructed the achievement of this goal.

In explaining his ideas Lucretius combined philosophic thought with explanations of the physical world which are an astonishing anticipation of modern scientific discovery. Accepting and developing the atomic theory first advanced by the Greek thinkers Leucippus and Democritus in the fifth century BC, he punctures our own conceit by showing us that now proven scientific theories which we have come to regard as an achievement of our own time were in fact first propounded more than two thousand years ago.

The poetry of Lucretius is a happy blend of logical argument with descriptive passages of great beauty, some of which are included in these translations. Time and again we find ourselves sharing the emotions aroused in him by scenes that have a timeless appeal to the heart.

Lucretius is not a poet whose verse can be dipped into as casually as the shorter Latin poems that follow. But those prepared to read his work with the time and effort that it requires and deserves, will find the effort richly rewarded.

First Principles

These dark imaginings that cloud the mind
Yield not to sunshine and the golden gleam
Of dawn's bright armament, but only to
A questioning of nature by ourselves,
Whereof the basic principle must be
That nothing ever, by some act divine,
Is born of nothing. For the human race
Is so beset by superstitious fears
That much of what occurs in heaven and earth
Without apparent cause is thought to be
Some god at work: but once we realise
That nothing out of nothing can be made,
Then we shall see our way more easily
In seeking explanations of events
Without recourse to supernaturals.
If things were causeless, nature could produce
One kind from any other seedlessly:
From ocean man would spring, and fish from land,
Birds would burst forth from heaven, wild beasts too
With cattle herds and flocks of sheep would share
Alike both desert waste and pastureland
Without discrimination of their birth,
Trees would have no consistency of fruit,
And each could bear another's. Were there not
Bodies to generate each single thing,
How could there be unchanging motherhood?
But as it is, because from their own seed
All things are born, the origin of each,
Whence it steps out upon the shores of light,
Is where its elemental substance lies
Inherent, and the reason everything
Must have its own progenitor is that
In each is fixed its own capacity.

And why is it, moreover, that we see
In spring the rose, in summer's heat the corn,
The vine at autumn's bidding bursting out,
If not because at their appointed time

52

The seeds of things conspire to bring them forth,
Each in its season, and the pregnant earth
Bears safe its tender burden to the light?
But if they came from nothing, they could spring
To sudden birth at any interval
Unseasonably, since there would not be
Parental seeds, whose fertile union
Could be prevented by the bar of time.
Besides, if things could rise from nothingness,
Time would be inessential to their growth:
Babes on a sudden would become young men,
And from the earth the trees would leap full-grown.
But manifestly this does not occur,
Since growth in everything is gradual
And rightly from its predetermined seed
Each keeps its race alive, and you can see
That each derives its growth and nourishment
From its intrinsic substance. Furthermore,
Without the year's assurances of rain
The land could not produce its gladsome crops,
And living things deprived of nourishment
Could not sustain themselves and propagate.
And so it is more easy to suppose
The self-same body shared by many things,
As words share letters, than for us to think
That anything exists without a cause.

And why, again, could nature not create
Men large enough to walk across the sea
Or tear apart great mountains with their hands,
Or conquer time to live from age to age,
If it be not that everything contains
Its own peculiar gene immutable,
Determining what it may reproduce?
So once again we cannot but admit
That nothing comes from nothing, since a seed
Is necessary to make each creature come
To birth and draw the tender breath of life.
And lastly, since the land we cultivate
Yields better crops than that which is untilled,

There must within the soil be elements
Which we, when we subject it to the plough,
And turn the fertile sods, stir up to birth:
If they did not exist, then you would see
All things improving of their own accord
Without the need of any toil from us.

And now my second principle, which is
That everything by nature is dissolved
Into its own components once again,
And nothing into nothing disappears.
If things were mortal in their every part,
Then we should see them perish all at once
Snatched from our sight, for nothing could prevent
The total loss of their constituents
And dissolution of their union.
But as it is, nature does not permit
The death of anything until it meets
With forcible disruption from without,
Or else disintegration from within.
Besides, if things are utterly destroyed,
And all their substance lost when time and age
Remove them from our sight, then whence is it
That Venus leads each race of living kind
Back to the light of life? Whence does the earth,
For all her skill, provide the nourishment
To give each race its increase? Whence again
Come all the springs and rivers from afar
To feed the ocean? Whence does outer space
Sustain the stars? For everything endowed
With mortal body would have been consumed
Long since in the infinity of time.
But if through ages past there have survived
Things out of which our universe is made
And evermore renewed, beyond a doubt
They must be blessed with immortality,
And so cannot revert to nothingness.
An equal force, moreover, would destroy
All things alike, were they not held in bond
By particles eternal, intertwined

In some degree of mutual embrace.
Were it not so, one touch would be enough
To cause destruction: not a thing would have
Enduring substance, but would fall apart
From any blow whatever. As it is,
Because the union of their elements
Is different, and the elements are made
Of matter everlasting, things remain
Inviolate in body till they meet
A force sufficient to dissolve in each
The combination of its particles.

So nothing comes to nothing: everything
At death returns unto its elements.
Although the rain that tumbles from the sky,
Our father, to the lap of mother earth
Appears to perish, yet the golden glow
Or corn springs up, the trees in every branch
Renew their green, and grow, and bear their fruit.
From rain, therefore, do man and beast alike
Derive their nourishment; to rain we owe
The towns rejoicing in the bloom of youth,
The leafy woodlands where on every side
Young birds are singing, nor without the rain
Would fattened cattle wearily lay down
Their bodies in the gladsome pastureland,
Nor would the milk come trickling snowy-white
From swollen udders, or the baby brood
On wobbly legs among the tender grass
Disport themselves in play, their little heads
Intoxicated with the milky wine.
And so, of all the things we see, not one
Is utterly destroyed, since nature makes
Each thing from something else, and undertakes
Creation only with the help of death.

Come now, since I have shown that nothing can
From nothing be created, and again
That nothing into nothing is recalled
Once brought to birth, lest still you start to doubt

My words, because component particles
Cannot be seen, I'll mention other things
Possessing substance, yet – you must concede –
Invisible. To start with, there's the wind,
Whose might, aroused to violent assault,
Lashes the ocean, puts the clouds to flight
And sinks huge ships, or rushes over land
Felling great trees in headlong hurricane,
And with its blast upon the mountain tops
Rending the forests: so with piercing howl
The wind storms on and roars its threat of doom.
Thus in the wind there are, you may be sure,
Bodies invisible, which sweep the sea,
The land and clouds of heaven, suddenly
In hurricane assembling to attack
And carry off their prey: their onward rush
And crop of havoc are as when a stream
Of gentle water quickly turns to flood,
Fed from high mountains after heavy rain
By raging torrents. Branches from the woods,
Even whole trees are hurled along with it:
Stout bridges are unable to withstand
The sudden onslaught, with such violence
The rain-fed river, swirling on its way,
Dashes against the piles, and with a roar
Deals out destruction, toppling giant stones
Beneath the waves, and overwhelming all
That dares obstruct the passage of the flood.
In suchlike manner must the blasts of wind
Be borne along: when, like a stream in spate,
They penetrate to any place at all
They thrust before them everything they meet,
Hurling them on in oft-renewed attack,
And sometimes in a whirlwind seizing them
To bear them upwards in a dizzy spin.
So I repeat, there are within the wind
Bodies unseen, because, as we have found,
They match exactly in behaviour
Great rivers, which are plainly visible.

And furthermore, we notice different smells
Though nothing can be seen to reach our nose:
Heat, cold and sound our eyes cannot observe,
Yet all, if they impinge upon our sense,
Must have corporeal substance; nothing can
Touch or be touched, that is not physical.
Again, when clothes are hung upon the shore,
Where break the waves of ocean, they grow damp,
But spread them in the sun and they will dry,
Though by what means the moisture penetrates
Or disappears, is hidden from our sight.
Therefore must we conclude it is dispersed
In particles too small for us to see.
A ring, moreover, after many years
Have come and gone with the returning sun,
Grows thin upon the finger wearing it:
The drip of water hollows out a stone,
The bent iron ploughshare imperceptibly
Grows smaller in the fields, and in the streets
We see how pavements have been trodden down
Beneath the footsteps of the multitude.
Bronze statues, too, beside the city gates
Hold out right hands that passers-by have worn
With many claspings. Yet in none of these
We see erosion till it has occurred,
And grudging nature has denied to sight
What particles are lost at any time.

De Rerum Natura, I, 146-321

The Philosopher Poet

Come, harken now, and clearly learn the rest.
I preach a doctrine difficult to see,
I know, yet hope is high within my breast
Of gaining glory by philosophy,
Implanting in my heart a tender love
For all the Muses, so that now with mind
Instilled with vigour, unrestrained I rove

Alone through distant Helicon, to find
Untrodden paths inviting to explore.
How wonderful to come upon fresh springs
And quench my thirst from their untasted store!
To pluck new flowers, whence never even kings
Were by the Muses crowned, and therewith make
A noble diadem to deck my brow!
First, since I teach great things, and strive to break
The fetters of religion, which till now
Have held the mind fast bound: and then as well
Because about a subject so obscure
I seek in simple poetry to tell,
Giving my explanation the allure
Of verse. For there is reason in this act:
Just as a doctor, when he tries to give
A boy the bitter wormwood, hides the fact,
Smearing the rim with honey from the hive,
That by the sweet deception which he sips
The unsuspecting lad may so be charmed
That, ere he knows, the drink is past his lips
And quaffed – yet by the trick he is not harmed
But rather is restored to health again
– So now do I, for bitter is this thing
To those who know it not, and hard to explain,
Since all recoil therefrom. I mean to sing
In verse mellifluous, and dip the whole
In the sweet honey that my muse supplies.
Hoping that thus I may attain my goal
And captivate your mind magician-wise,
While you unveil all Nature's mysteries
And learn the shape of everything that is.

De Rerum Natura, I, 921-950

The Quiet Mind

Pleasant it is, when on the sea's expanse
Gales lash the waters, to be safe ashore
Watching the toils of others; not because

There's any pleasure in the sufferings
Of other men, but rather in the sight
Of tribulations you need not endure.
'Tis pleasant, too, to sit above the plain
And see the embattled armies come to grips
While you are safe and have no part in it.
But best of all, to dwell in cloistered calm
Upon the lofty ramparts which the wise
Have by their teaching built for you, wherefrom
You can look down and see your fellow men
Aimlessly searching for the path of life
On every side, contending mind with mind
And rank with rank in effort night and day
To be the richest or most powerful.
Oh, the blind hearts, the paltry minds of men!
How dark the night, how great the dangers are
In this brief span of life! Do you not see
That Nature cries aloud for nothing else
Save only that the body feel no pain,
The mind be carefree, innocent of fear,
And knowing naught but happiness? And so
Our body's needs, we see, are few indeed,
None but those things that keep it free of pain.
Despite the pleasure luxury can bring,
Yet who can say that Nature really needs
– And sometimes one is happier without –
Gold statuettes of youths throughout the house,
In whose right hand is held a fiery torch
To brighten evening banquets; or a home
Glinting wih gold and silver, or again
Gold-fretted rafters echoing the lute,
When after all, outstretched beneath the trees
Upon the yielding grass beside a stream
At little cost our bodies can enjoy
Sweet relaxation, which is sweeter still
On sunny days when summer spreads a mat
Of flowers on the greenness of the sward?
Nor does it profit you, when sick you lie
With burning fever, if you toss and turn
On rich-embroidered sheets or purple couch:

The fever lasts as long as if you lay
In poor man's raiment on a humbler bed.
Since therefore in our bodily estate
Treasure, high birth and even kingly fame
Avail us nothing, so one must suppose
The mind as well from suchlike vanities
Can nothing gain: unless perchance you think
That superstitions and the fear of death
In terror fly, leaving your heart serene,
When you behold your legions in the field
Swarming in mock manoeuvres, reinforced
By great reserves and ranks of cavalry,
All strongly armed and spoiling for the fight.
But if we recognise how ludicrous
And laughable are such ideas, and that
The fears, the cares that dog our mortal steps
Themselves fear not the clash of sword on sword,
The cruel spear, but mingle unabashed
With kings and potentates, without regard
For gleaming gold or raiment purple-bright,
Then can you doubt that these imaginings
Are subject to our reason? All the more
Must this be so, when life is labour spent
Amid the shadows: just as children quake
With terror in the dark at everything,
So we at times in broadest daylight fear
Things that in truth are no more terrible
Than darkling bogies of a little child.
To pierce this gloom, to rid our minds of fear
We need, not sunlight and the shafts of day,
But observation of the natural world
And thought about the laws that govern it.

De Rerum Natura, II, 1-61

The Invisible Atom

Nor need you at this juncture wonder why,
When all the particles composing things

Are in perpetual motion, yet the whole
Appears to be completely motionless,
Save when the body of some other thing
Impels its movement. For the nature of
The particles lies buried far beneath
The range of our sensation, so that if
You cannot see them, neither can you see
Them move: still less, since even what we see
Will often hide its movement from our eyes
When at a distance from us. Woolly flocks,
For instance, as they graze upon a hill
The fertile pasture, slowly shamble on
Where'er the grass fresh-hung with diamond dew
Invites each one, and little lambs, milk-full,
Gambol and butt their heads in friendly play:
Yet from afar 'tis nothing but a blur,
A patch of white upon the green hillside.
Again, when mighty legions fill the plain
In mock attack and mimicry of war,
Their glitter rises upward to the sky
And bright with bronze is all the land around:
Earth shakes beneath the thunder of their feet,
Their shouting smites the mountains, whence in turn
It echoes to the starry firmament,
The cavalry wheel round, and suddenly
Burst forth to shock the centre of the field,
Yet high upon the hills there is a spot
Whence everything appears to be at rest,
The battlefield is but a distant gleam.

De Rerum Natura, II, 308-332

Fear Death?

Death, then, is nothing to us, and need not
One jot concern us, since the mind of man
Itself is mortal. If we suffered naught
In times gone by, wherein from every side
The Carthaginians surged into the fray,

When underneath the lofty coasts of space
The world was shaken by the din of war
And all things trembled, while it yet remained
Uncertain who would gain the mastery
And rule on land and sea the human race
– So, when we are no more, when body parts
From soul, whose union makes us what we are,
You may be sure that not a single thing
Can then befall us or bestir our sense
When we are dead – no, not if land and sea,
Or sea and sky, should then be intermixed.
And if our mind and faculty of soul
Have any kind of feeling once divorced
From flesh and blood, yet it can nothing be
To us, for whom existence is derived
From soul and body bound in union.
Again, if time to come beyond our death
Should gather flesh and blood to recreate
Our present body, and once more bestow
The light of life upon us, that event
Would not at all affect us, once the chain
Of memory had suffered severance.
Why, even now how little do we care
For those who once we were in ages past:
For, looking back upon the infinite
Expanse of time gone by, the manifold
Motions of matter, you might well believe
That these same seeds of which we now are made
Could often in the past have been disposed
Exactly as they are in us today;
Yet have we no remembrance of the fact,
Because an end of life has intervened
And all the moving particles have gone
Their several ways divorced from human sense.

For if a man is doomed to suffer grief
And pain, he must exist at that same time
When suffering is due: but seeing that
Death renders this impossible, and bars
Existence to the one on whom these ills

Are poised to fall, you may be very sure
That there is naught in death for us to fear,
Nor can a mortal feel unhappiness
Who is no more: when once immortal death
Has stolen mortal life, he differs not
One whit from him that never has been born.
Thus should you see a man bewail his lot
Because when dead his body in the grave
Will putrefy, or perish in the flames,
Or be consumed by hungry carnivores,
Then you must know he lacks the ring of truth;
Some hidden pang is gnawing at his heart,
However much he may protest he knows
There can be no sensation after death.
For what this man professes to believe
And why, methinks he does not truly grant,
Nor can his reason bear to contemplate
Himself from living utterly removed,
But clings unwittingly to the belief
That something of him somehow will survive.
For when in life each man's imagining
Pictures the day that birds of prey or beasts
Will rend his flesh, he grieves but for himself;
Unable to divorce his conscious mind
From outcast body, which he deems to be
His very self, he stands beside the corpse
Defiling it with his own consciousness.
Thus he repines that he was mortal born,
And does not realise that in true death
No other self is left alive to mourn
His passing, or to suffer when he sees
His corpse desmembered or consumed by fire.
For if in death it is an evil thing
To be thus rended by the jaws of beasts,
I doubt if one would feel a lesser pain
To have oneself committed to the flames
And roast upon the pyre, or suffocate
Embalmed in honey, and grow stiff with cold
Upon the surface of some icy rock,
Or lie beneath a crushing weight of earth.

'No more,' men say, 'no more your happy home
Will greet you now, no more the best of wives
And children sweet will run to claim the first
Fond kiss, and touch your heart with happiness
Too deep for words. No longer can you now
Enjoy prosperity in your affairs
Or shield your loved ones. O unhappy man,
From whom, alas, one miserable day
Has taken all the rich rewards of life!'
In saying this, they fail to add besides
'Neither does any longing for such things
Remain with you.' Which thought if they could grasp,
And match it in their words, they would dispel
A load of fear and anguish from their hearts.
'Though you indeed may sleep the sleep of death,
Relieved for evermore of every kind
Of woe, we stood beside the awesome pyre
And wept our eyes out inconsolably
To see the flames consume you. Not for us
Can any day extinguish in our hearts
The sorrow that can never be assuaged.'
Of him that thus complains we must inquire,
If sleep and rest eternal at the last
Become our destiny, then what in this
Is so exceeding sad that anyone
Should pine away in never-ending grief?

And there's another thing men often do
When seated round the table: glass in hand,
And garland on their brow, they from the heart
Exclaim, 'Too fleeting is this festive hour
For mortal men; too soon it will be past,
And we can never bring it back again'
– As if in death they'll suffer nothing worse,
Poor souls, than raging thirst, or feel the lack,
When that day comes, of anything at all.
For when both mind and body are at rest
In sleep, no man then longs for self and life:
For all we know, that sleep may never end,
But still we feel no yearning for ourselves.

64

Yet at such times the elements of life
Stray through our limbs not far removed from sense,
Prepared for action when the waking man
Springs back from sleep to consciousness again.
Much less must death be reckoned, then, to us
(If less can be than that we see as naught),
For when we die, the stuff of which we're made
Is scattered in confusion greater far
Than in our sleep, and none will then awake
To rise again, when once the chilly end
Of mortal life has overtaken him.

Suppose that Nature suddenly spoke up
And reprimanded one of us like this:
'Mortal, how comes it death can mean so much
To you, that you excessively bewail
Its advent? Why the groaning and the tears?
For if your life has been a happy one,
And all its pleasures have not trickled through
Untasted, as if poured into a sieve,
Why not retire now sated with the feast
And with a tranquil heart, you idiot,
Grasp at the chance of trouble-free repose?
If on the other hand the fruit you've plucked
Has gone to waste, and life is odious,
Why seek to add to it, when what you add
Is doomed to perish likewise unenjoyed?
Is it not better you should make an end
Of life and toil? For there is nothing more
I can devise or find to please you: all
Is just the same as ever, even though
Your body is not withered by the years,
Your limbs unwearied, everything remains
Eternally unchanged – yes, even though
You lived to conquer all the centuries
And had the gift of immortality.'

What can we answer, save that Nature's charge
Is soundly based, and that the cause she pleads
Has truth upon its side? And then again,

Should someone older and of high estate
Extravagantly mourn his coming death,
Could she not justifiably exclaim
In sharp rebuke: 'Stop snivelling, you fool,
And curb your grumbles. All the rich rewards
Of life you have received, and now your time
Is come. But since invariably you spurn
The things you have, and covet what you lack,
Your life yet incomplete and unenjoyed
Has slipped away, and death has unawares
Crept up on you before you've had your fill
And, satisfied, are ready to depart.
So now relinquish all that you possess,
Which younger generations should enjoy,
And tranquilly surrender to the years
At last, for so necessity commands.'
Rightly again, I think, would Nature plead
And rightly chide, for always must the old
Give way to youth, and from the death of one
Another one draw life; and none goes down
Into the pit and darkest Tartarus.
Always there must be matter out of which
May grow new generations, which in turn
Must end their days and follow you to death,
Passing away like those that went before.
This chain, whereby one thing is brought to birth
By something else, is endless, and to none
Is life a freehold gift, but only leased.
Look back once more and see how ages past
Of endless time, before we saw the light,
Have nothing meant to us; these Nature holds
Before our eyes to show, as in a glass,
The face of time when we are dead and gone.
Does this seem sad to you, or terrible?
Could any sleep bestow a greater peace?

De Rerum Natura, III, 830-977

66

The Lost Calf

Come now and learn the origin of things,
What makes them what they are, all different
In outward aspect and component form:
The difference is not in looks alone,
That some are unlike others, but that all
Are of their nature quite dissimilar.
And little wonder when, as I have shown,
Their name is legion and their multitude
Past measuring, and so beyond a doubt
They cannot all be like in size and shape.
Take what you will – mankind, the scaly shoals
Of silent swimmers, or the fattened herds,
Wild animals, or birds of every kind
That haunt the pleasant spots where water is,
Springs, river banks and lakes, or stir the glades
Of distant forests with their fluttering:
Take any one from others of its kind
And you will find it differs from the rest,
For otherwise the young could never know
Their mother, nor the mother know her young,
And yet this recognition is no less
With animals than with the race of men.
Oft at the threshold of some stately shrine
A calf has fallen, sacrificed before
The incense-burning altar, breathing out
Hot streams of life-blood from his wounded breast;
But through the pastures green his mother goes
Bereft, and finding pressed into the earth
His cloven footprints, searches everywhere
Seeking in vain the child that she has lost,
Standing awhile to fill with her lament
The leafy glade, and every now and then
Returning to her stall, her heart transfixed
With yearning for her young. No longer now
The tender willows and the dewy sward,
The river gliding level with its banks,
Can bring her joy or ease her sudden grief;
No other calf in that rich pastureland

67

Can soothe her pang, or bring oblivion
Of suffering, so desperate her need
Of something that she knows to be her own.

De Rerum Natura, II, 333-366

Escape?

Could men but understand, when weight of care
Wearies the mind, the cause that gives it birth,
Filling their heart with such a mass of woe,
They would not spend their lives as all too oft
We see them do, not knowing what they want
And ever seeking some new pleasure-ground,
As if to shed their burden by the change.
See how the great man, tired of life at home,
Quits his palatial house to go abroad,
Then, finding things no better, suddenly
Comes back again. Next, to his country lodge
He drives his ponies at a breakneck speed,
For all the world as if there was a fire
To be extinguished: but when he arrives
No sooner is his foot upon the steps
Than he is bored, or hurries off to bed,
Hoping that sleep will help him to forget,
Or even rushes citywards again.
Thus every man attempts a self-escape
That cannot be, and hates himself because
He does not know whence comes his malady.
Could he but see this plainly, each of us
Would soon let private trivia go hang
And study first the universe of things
And what they are, for what remains in doubt
Is not the nature of a single hour,
But time eternal, since it is in this
That mortal man in destined to endure
Whatever may await him after death.
Again, what evil lust for life is it
That conquers us when danger is at hand?
The end awaits us all, beyond a doubt:

Death knows no by-pass, and it must be faced.
Besides, we change not our environment,
And no new pleasures come from living on;
Yet what we covet seems of paramount
Importance to us, if we have it not,
And when we gain it, then comes something else
That we must have, and so unendingly
The thirst for life remains unsatisfied.
Remember, too, that we can never know
What fortune time may bring, what circumstance
May challenge us, or how it will result:
Nor by the prolongation of our life
Do we reduce the time we shall be dead
Or win subtraction from mortality.
Therefore live on as long as you may please
From age to age – still everlasting death
Will lie in wait, and he that dies today
Will not endure a shorter nothingness
Than he that perished months or years ago.

De Rerum Natura, III, 1053-1094

In the Steps of Epicurus

He, then, it is whose footprints now I tread,
Tracking in words his arguments, to show
That those same rules by which all things are made
Must govern them as long as they exist,
And time's great laws can never be repealed.
For instance, first of all, as I have proved,
The nature of the soul is at the start
Born of its native body, and cannot
Survive intact throughout eternity,
Though dreams will oft delude us, when in sleep
We see once more a man bereft of life.
And next the order of my argument
Has led me to the point where I must show
The universe had, too, its day of birth
And has a mortal body: also, how
The gathering of its constituents

Produced the earth, the sky, the sea, the stars,
The sun and moon; and then, which living things
Sprang up on earth, and which have never been,
How men first came to give such things a name
And so communicate in diverse tongues;
And how, inspired with terror of the gods,
They came to consecrate throughout the world
Shrines, lakes and groves, altars and images.
And furthermore, by what controlling force
Nature directs the journeys of the sun
And of the errant moon, I will expound,
Lest we should think that of their own accord
From year to year they freely go their way
Twixt heaven and earth, disposed to swell the growth
Of crops and living creatures, or suppose
They roll along by agency divine.

De Rerum Natura, V, 55-81

The Birth of Superstition

And now what led great nations to believe
In deities, to fill their cities full
Of sacred altars, and to institute
The solemn rites that flourish still today
In mighty states and places of renown,
Whence even now originates the dread
That causes men to raise throughout the world
New shrines of gods, full-thronged on holy days
– All this in words is easily explained.
For even then, in bygone centuries,
The gods appeared in superhuman form
To men in waking visions, and still more
In dreams, with bodies of a wondrous size.
To these, sensation was attributed
By men, for they were seen to move their limbs
And heard to speak with voice magnificent
To match their noble mien and mighty strength.
They took them for immortal, too, because
Their apparitions constantly recurred

In form unchanged, and more especially
Because they did not think that those endowed
With strength so great could yield to any force.
Thus they believed them happier by far
Than mortal men, because not one of them
Was ever troubled by the fear of death,
And in their dreams, besides, they saw the gods
Perform so many wondrous miracles
Without apparent effort. Furthermore,
They watched the motions of the firmament
And seasons coming round from year to year,
But could not understand the reason why
Such things occurred; thus they resorted to
Attributing these marvels to the gods,
Whose will they held to be omnipotent.
They fixed their habitation in the sky,
Since through the sky it is that night and moon
Are seen to roll along – moon, day and night,
And night's grim portents, starry wanderers
That shoot across the heavens, and flying fires,
Clouds, sunshine, rain and snow, wind, lightning, hail,
Swift thunderclaps and rumbles menacing.

O wretched men, who to the gods ascribed
Such happenings, and added wrath divine!
What groans they brought themselves, what woe to us,
What tears to generations yet unborn!
There's nothing good in being often seen
Turning, head veiled, towards the sacred stone,
Or going up the steps of sanctuaries,
There to prostrate one's frame upon the floor
With palms outspread before the holy shrines,
Or sprinkling altars with the streaming blood
Of quadrupeds, or piling vow on vow,
But rather in our learning to observe
All things with quiet mind. For when we look
Up at the skies of this great universe
And see the void of heaven set above
The twinkling stars, and when we think besides
About the courses of the sun and moon,

Then in our hearts, already sore oppressed
With other woes, springs up this further fear
To raise its head, that over us perhaps
There may be gods omnipotent who set
The shining stars upon their changing course.
For reason's poverty impels the mind
To wonder if the world had any birth
Or will have any end, until which time
Its walls can still continue to endure
Eternally, and gliding on defy
The onslaughts of immeasurable time.

Whose heart, moreover, does not miss a beat
In terror of the gods, who does not shrink
In dread, when lightning strikes the torrid earth
And thunderclaps go rumbling through the sky?
Do not the nations tremble then, and proud
Kings clutch their limbs in fear of wrath divine,
Lest retribution may have come at last
For some unholy deed or haughty word?
And when, again, at sea a mighty gale
Drives some great admiral across the deep
With all his legions and his elephants,
Does he not seek to pacify the gods
With vows, and pray in terror that the gale
May cease and change to favourable winds
– In vain, for caught in raging hurricane
He still is swept upon the shoals of death?
So thoroughly does some mysterious power
Obliterate things human and, it seems,
Contemptuously grind man's panoply,
Fair rods and cruel axes, into dust.
And finally, when underneath our feet
The whole earth rocks and cities tumble down
From sudden shock, or totter, is it then
Surprising that man scorns his puny self
And puts his faith in gods omnipotent
Whose wondrous strength controls the universe?

De Rerum Natura, V, 1161-1240

Catullus

Valerius Catullus was born at Verona in 87 BC. His father be-
queathed him considerable wealth, which the poet proceeded to
dissipate in Roman society life. After visiting Bithynia in an
unsuccessful attempt to help his finances, he returned to Rome,
where he managed to live comfortably enough, having a house in
the city and country estates at Sirmio and Tibur, the present-day
Tivoli. He died in about 47 BC. Of his poems 116 survive, some of
which are lyrical, others epigrammatic. The 'Lesbia' of his love
affair was almost certainly Clodia, the wife of Q. Metellus Celer,
and sister of Cicero's enemy, Publius Clodius.

The Sparrow – 1

Sparrow, my little darling's pet,
On whose sweet breast you stay,
Who lets you nip her finger-tip
And loves with you to play.

My lady fair enjoys with you
Such charming recreation;
When sorrow's dart has pierced her heart
You are her consolation.

How well I know, when passion ebbs,
That cruel pang of grief!
Would that I too could play with you
And find the same relief.

II

73

The Sparrow – 2

The darling of my darling's heart,
Her little sparrow's dead,
Than whom to lose she'd rather choose
To give her eyes instead.

Her sweetling pet was he, that knew
Her as a child its mother,
And chirping hither, chirping thither,
Flew back to her, no other.

But back from you, O cruel Death,
There's no return to living
Out of the gloom where you consume
All beauty unforgiving.

Poor little sparrow, snatched away
To Death's eternal sleeping!
Poor girl, who cries with lovely eyes
All swollen red with weeping!

III

Love's Arithmetic

Let's live and love while yet we may,
My Lesbia: all the things they say,
Those crabbed old gossips, let's agree,
Aren't worth a farthing – what care we?
Each night the sun goes down, each morn
Another bright new day is born,
But when we quench our puny light,
Comes endless sleep, eternal night.
So kiss me, Lesbia, I implore,
A thousand times, a hundred more,
Another thousand, with again
A hundred kisses in their train,
And even after these I will

74

Demand eleven hundred still,
Whereat we'd better cease to tot
And mix together all the lot,
Lest envious eyes should keep the count
And grudge my lips the full amount.

V

Verbal Contract

There's none, she says, that she would wed
But me, though Jove himself besought her.
Words! Will they live when passion's fled?
Nay, let her pen her pledge instead
– In empty air and running water.

LXX

Bitter Sweet

To such a pitch of lunacy, my Lesbia, am I brought
By you, my mental processes so hopelessly distraught,
That though you were an angel, still I could not wish you well,
Yet I'd have to go on loving you, if you were black as hell.

LXXXV

Sirmio

O Sirmio, pearl of isles and almost-isles
That float in Neptune's arms on stilly lakes
Or mighty seas, how gladly I return,
How thankfully, scarce crediting that I
Have left Bithynia's plains and come back safe
To see you once again! Ah, what can be
More blissful than to ease the troubled mind
Of worry's burden, and arriving home
Weary of labour in a foreign land,

75

To rest upon the bed so long desired?
How amply this atones for all my toil!
Hail and rejoice, my lovely Sirmio!
Be happy also, ripples on the lake,
And laugh with every chuckle you possess.

XXXI

NOTE: Sirmio, now Sermione, lies on the southern shore of what is
now Lake Garda. Catullus had returned in 56 BC from a civil service
job in Asia Minor.

Paralysis

He's more than superhuman who
Can bear to sit in front of you
And look you in the face, and hear
Your lovely laugh. When I am near,
Your beauty, Lesbia, I confess,
Reduces me to senselessness:
My tongue is tied, the vital flame
Burns low within my feeble frame,
My ears go buzz as hearing dies,
And darkness falls upon my eyes.

LI

Retirement

You see that skiff, my friends? That little boat
Can claim she was the fastest thing afloat:
No other craft propelled by sail or oar
Could match her, as the Adriatic shore
And the Aegean isles will testify,
Who in her prime beheld her passing by.
Great Rhodes and grim Propontis knew her too,
And that wild Pontic bay whereupon there grew
The trees that formed the timbers of her frame,
Which whispered to the oarsmen whence they came.

76

And as this little craft of mine can tell,
Amastris and Cytorus knew her well
And know her still, for how could they forget
There she was built, there first her blades were wet,
And thence she carried me through many a strait,
However dangerous, inviolate.
It mattered not, cross wind on any tack,
Or with the breeze to help me at my back,
Never was need for her endangered master
To beg the gods to save him from disaster,
Until at last she finished with the sea
And came to share this limpid lake with me.

All that was long ago that I have told:
Now laid up here she peacefully grows old,
And dedicates this aging frame of hers
To those twin gods who guard all mariners.

IV

NOTE: Catullus had sailed his boat home at the end of his service in
Bithynia. The reference in the last line is to Castor and Pollux.

Horace

Horace (Q. Horatius Flaccus) was born in 65 BC, the son of a freedman – that is, an emancipated slave – who devoted all his financial resources to his education in Rome. Horace quickly achieved fame and fortune as a poet, gaining the friendship as well as the patronage of the wealthy Maecenas, and in his later years even receiving honours at the hands of the emperor Augustus, whom he named as his heir at his death in 8 BC. The Sabine farm mentioned in his verses was presented to Horace by Maecenas about 34 BC.

Self Defence

> The virtuous, the innocent
> Need never, Fuscus, go equipped
> With Moorish lance for armament,
> Or bow and arrows poison-tipped,
> Though to the torrid Afric shore
> He travels, the unfriendly land
> Of Caucasus, or e'en explore
> Hydaspes' legendary strand.
>
> While in the Sabine woods I strayed
> And sang of love and Lalage,
> Crossing my boundary unafraid
> I met a wolf, who turned to flee.
> Defenceless I, and yet I faced
> A brute that might have had its home
> In Daunia's forests, or the waste
> Of Juba's land, where lions roam.

Set me in climes wherein the trees
Stand unrefreshed on barren plain
By cooling breath of summer breeze,
Where mist and darkling heavens reign,
Or where the sun too close above
Burns desert sand – whate'er your choice
Still Lalage shall be my love,
Her gentle laugh, her gentle voice.

Odes, I, 22

Pyrrha

What scent-sprayed youngster, Pyrrha, presses
His slender form to your caresses
In some secluded rosy lair?
For whom is now your golden hair
Entwined with artless artistry?
How many times his trust will he,
Betrayed by gods and you, bewail
And watch amazed the darkling gale
Lashing the waves! Poor innocent,
Who now enjoys in sweet content
His golden girl, and thinks she is
A darling always, always his.
Your fickle breeze he little knows!
What anguish lies ahead for those
You dazzle fleetingly, but who
Have yet to learn the real you!
For me, a tablet on the wall
Of Neptune's temple tells it all,
Where I have hung my dripping wet
Old sailor togs, lest I forget,
Almighty ocean-god, the day
You rescued Pyrrha's castaway.

Odes, I, 5

NOTE: The last six lines refer to the custom of hanging com-
memorative tablets and dedicatory offerings in the temple of
Neptune, in thanksgiving for survival at sea.

79

Warming Words

See how Soracte's peak up there is white
With depth of snow, and how the stricken trees
Bend in the woods beneath their heavy load,
While river flow is halted by the ice.
Come, pile the logs in plenty on the fire,
Putting the cold to flight; be generous,
My friend, and fetch the four-year vintage wine.
Leave all the rest to be the gods' concern,
Who calm the raging winds and stormy sea
Till ancient ash and cypress shake no more.

Seek not to ask what things may lie ahead,
But count as credit all the days that fate
Bestows on you. You're in the bloom of youth,
Grey hairs and peevishness are far away:
Do not despise the joys of love and dance.
Now is the time when pleasures of the town
Should summon you, soft whispers in the night
At lovers' meetings, when at hide-and-seek
The welcome laughter of a pretty girl
Betrays her secret hiding-place, and when
A pledge of love is stolen from an arm
Or from a finger failing to resist.

Odes, I, 9

Contentment

Peace the poor sailor, sorely tried
By storm, prays Neptune to provide,
When moon is hid by inky cloud
And friendly stars are not allowed
    To be his guide.

Thracians with war-like ardour burn,
And yet it is for peace they yearn,
For peace the Median[1] archer sighs:
Jewels nor gold that precious prize
    Can ever earn.

No royal bounty, Grosphus, or
Enforcer of the rule of law
Can quell the riots that you find,
Circling the ceiling of your mind,
 The cares that gnaw.

The man who is the modest heir
To one small piece of silverware
Upon his humble board, lives right:
No fear disturbs his sleep at night,
 No greed is there.

Why let our aspirations grow
When life's so short? Why should we go
To foreign climes where days are hot?
We may escape the cold, but not
 Ourselves, you know.

However fast the ship you sail,
Vile care will clamber o'er the rail;
The fleetest fawn, the swiftest steed
Can't match her, nor the hustling speed
 Of eastern gale.

He that enjoys the sun today
Cares not tomorrow may be grey;
Smiling at all life's miseries
He knows that nothing perfect is
 In every way.

Achilles[2] was too early dead,
Old age Tithonus[3] surfeited:
Some die too early, some too late,
And what she has denied you, Fate
 Gives me instead.

Sicilian cows around you moo,
And countless sheep you number too;
Your racehorse whinnies in her stall,
Your woollens, double-dyed, are all
 Of purple hue.

Yet Fate, behaving honestly,
Allots a little farm to me:
By poetry my heart is stirred,
And hatred of the common herd
    For company.

Odes, II, 16

NOTES:
[1] The Medes were poetically equated with the Parthians, whose archery prowess was proverbial.
[2] Achilles was killed in his prime by Paris, with a shot fired at his heel, the only vulnerable part of his body.
[3] Tithonus was a handsome Trojan prince with whom the goddess Aurora fell in love. She granted his wish to be made immortal, but as he had failed to ask for eternal youth, he became unbearably decrepit, and begged Aurora to end his misery. Since he could not die, she changed him into a cicada.

Eheu, Fugaces…

Alas, alas, dear Postumus,
How rapidly the years are flying!
No pious worship can delay
Old age's wrinkles on their way
Or halt the certainty of dying.

My friend, were you to sacrifice
Three hundred bulls each day life gave you,
When his dark ocean can subdue
Great giants thrice the size of you[1]
Why should relentless Pluto save you?[2]

All men whom bounteous earth supports
Must on that sea one day be sailing:
Rustic or king, poor man or rich,
It matters not to Pluto which,
For wealth with him is unavailing.

In vain the bloody god of war
Or Adriatic storms may spare us;
In vain, when summer days are done
And autumn comes, we seek to shun
The unhealthy southern winds that scare us.

Where black Cocytus's sluggish stream[3]
Along its errant course is flowing,
Where Sisyphus heaves his rock uphill[4]
And Danaus's daughters fill
Their endless pails[5] – that's where we're going.

Your land, your home, the wife you love
Must all be left: those trees you've tended
Will not go with the lord they've known
So short a time. Cypress alone
Will follow you when life is ended[6].

Those vintages your heir will drink
Which, locked away, you've long been storing,
And he'll deserve them, spilling wine
Nobler than when the pontiffs dine,
To stain your lovely marble flooring.

Odes, II, 14

NOTES:
1. The text mentions two giants, Geryon, who had three bodies and heads, and Tityus, whose frame covered nine acres.
2. God of the underworld.
3. A river in Hades formed from the tears of the condemned.
4. A king of Corinth who murdered travellers, and was condemned to roll a huge rock up a hill, only to see it roll down again to the bottom.
5. Forty-nine of the fifty daughters slew their husbands on their wedding night because of a prophecy that their father would be killed by his son-in-law. They were punished in Hades by having to pour water endlessly into bottomless buckets. Lynceus, husband of Hypermnestra, the only daughter who had refused to obey her father's order, killed Danaus, and so fulfilled the prophecy.
6. The cypress was sacred to Pluto, and coffins were made from its wood.

Carpe Diem

Ask not what fate the gods decree,
Leuconoë, for you and me:
It's wrong to do so, or to look
For answers in astrology.

Better to bear unfaltering
Whatever each new day may bring,
Whether this winter be your last
Which sets the ocean buffeting
The rocks of the Tyrrhenian shore,
Or whether you'll have many more.

If you are wise, you'll drink the wine
That's locked behind your cellar door:
When life's so short, you must not seek
To nurse long hopes, for while we speak
Time flies. So pluck your fruit today
And don't expect too much next week.

Odes, I, 11

The Rat Race

I wonder why, Maecenas, there is not a person who
With the life that he has chosen, or just happens to pursue,
Is contented, rather praising men of different careers?
'Lucky traders!' says the soldier, overburdened by his years
And frail from length of service: but the trader, when at sea
He is tossed by a tornado, says 'A soldier's life for me!
'There's a battle, and in moments he will either win the day
'Or be speedily despatched.' And the solicitor will say
That he'd like to be a farmer, when he hears a client knock
At his doorstep very early, ere the farmer hears the cock;
While the farmer, summoned townwards to negotiate a loan,
Finds the city-dweller's happiness much greater than his own.
I could quote a host of others, but I will not be a bore,
So I'll spare you, and proceed to the conclusion that I draw:

If a god should on a sudden by a miracle appear,
Saying, 'Lo, to grant your wishes in a twinkling I am here!
'You, the soldier, be a trader! Be a farmer, man of law!
'All change and off you go, then! Well, what are you waiting
     for?'
Such a chance of being happy would, I wager, be refused,
And an irritated Jupiter could surely be excused
For his vehement assurance that if they should try again
To entreat his intervention, they will pray to him in vain.

Let me not be superficial like the laughter of a fool
(Though in laughter can be truth, just as sometimes in a school
The rudiments of knowledge are more quickly seen to pass
Under cover of a biscuit in a kindergarten class):
All the same, a truce to jesting – let's be serious for now.
The chap that turns the furrow with the metal of his plough,
The soldier, and the sailor who goes venturing afar
Upon the seven seas, and this old rogue behind the bar
– If you ask them what they work for, their reply will be the
     same,
That security and leisure in retirement is their aim
When old age has come upon them and their granary is full,
For they emulate the ant, who will laboriously pull
As much as she is able in her tiny mouth to take
To swell the little pile that she has set herself to make.
Well she knows there is a future that must be provided for,
And when the sad year-ending comes, she ventures out no
     more
But lives on what her prudence has already brought to eat,
While you, oblivious of winter cold or summer heat,
Go braving fire and sword, and all the perils of the sea,
Lest someone else should overtop your own prosperity.

What good to you's a mass of gold and silver that you hide
Buried in secret? 'Ah, but then, if I were to divide
My fortune, it would be reduced to pence.' Yet if you keep
It undistributed, what sort of beauty has your heap?
Though a hundred thousand bushels stand upon your
     threshing-floor,
Your stomach won't be capable of holding any more

85

Than mine, just as the man who bears the picnic haversack
Receives no more than those who carry nothing on their back.
Or say, for him that lives within the bounds nature allows,
What matter if it is a hundred acres that he ploughs
And not a thousand? 'But,' you say, 'how very nice it is
To help oneself like this from such enormous quantities!'
Yet if we have the right to take the same amount as you
From our small bins, why praise your store as highly as you
      do?
It is as if you said, 'I must insist on filling up
From some great river,' when you need no more than one
      small cup
Or jug of water, which a little brook could well supply:
So those it takes inordinate amounts to satisfy
Are swept away when Aufidus destroys its banks in flood,
While moderates are saved – and drink their water free from
      mud.

Yet many, led astray by greed's deception, will profess,
'You cannot have enough: you're judged by how much you
      possess.'
With such a man, what's to be done? One can but tell him to
Enjoy his misery, if this is what he wants to do
– Like the story of the miserly Athenian millionaire
Who scorned unpopularity, and said 'What do I care
If people choose to hiss me, when at home I can applaud
As I open up my cashbox and inspect my little hoard?'
Why laugh at thirsty Tantalus, who vainly tried to drink
Elusive streams? The parallel is closer than you think
To you, if you but change the name. With mouth agape you sleep
Upon the moneybags that you have gathered in a heap,
And yet they might be sacrosanct, so resolute your heart
To touch them not, enjoying them as if they're works of art.
Don't you know what money's worth, then, or the things that
      it can buy?
Bread, greens, a little wine – in fact the things that you deny
To nature at the price of pain. Or do you so delight
To lie awake and faint with fear, to spend each day and night
In dread of burglars, fire, or slaves who'll plunder you and
      flee?
Are these the sweets of wealth? If so, it's poverty for me.

'But when you have to go to bed because you have a chill,
Or for some other reason you are feeling rather ill,
You have someone there to nurse you, make a poultice for
     your pain,
Or go and fetch a doctor who will make you well again
And restore you to your loved ones.' But they care not if you
     die!
Wife, son, boys, girls, friends, neighbours – all detest you
     equally:
Can you wonder, when you value money far away above
All else, that you do not receive or merit any love?
Would it really, if you tried to keep them closer to your heart,
The folks that you are blessed with at no effort on your part,
Be such an uphill struggle to retain your kith and kin
As you might have in the Campus if you trained an ass to win?

So let there be a limit to the wealth you would acquire,
And when you've put a little by and gained your heart's desire,
Let fear of poverty recede, and set yourself to bring
Your labours to an end, in case you do the very thing
Ummidius did. The tale is brief: such riches he possessed
He used a rule to count them, yet so miserly, he dressed
No better than a slave. Until he drew his final breath
He was tortured by the fear he'd be a pauper at his death;
But he perished from the hatchet of a brave freedwoman, who
Outdid Queen Clytemnestra and divided him in two.
'What then do you suggest? That I should simply spend and
     spend?'
Oh come, you're putting opposites together end to end.
When I criticise your meanness, I do not of course suggest
You become a worthless wastrel. Moderation is the best.
There is a mean in everything; beyond it lies excess
On either side, whose boundaries the good will not trangress.

Returning to the question that I posed when I began,
Why contentment with his lot is never felt by any man,
It's avarice that makes him praise each calling but his own,
Or even feel upset when someone else's goat has grown
To yield more milk than his. For he is not content to match
The poor majority of men, but sets himself to catch

First one and then another. When you're running such a race
There is always someone richer you are trying to outpace.
As when the coursing chariots from the starting-gate have sped,
The driver presses on the heels of horses still ahead
With no regard for those he has already caught and passed
Who, galloping behind him, are contenders to be last.
And so we find but rarely any man who will admit
His life has been a happy one, and when it's time to quit
At last, is quite content to thank his host and say goodbye.
As one who has enjoyed the best of hospitality.

Satires, I, 1

Ovid

Ovid (P. Ovidius Naso), born in 43 BC, was the last poet of the Augustan age. A prolific writer, he shocked many contemporaries, including the Emperor himself, by his uninhibited *Ars Amatoria*. For reasons which remain uncertain, he was banished by Augustus to Tomi, on the Black Sea, where he died in AD 17.

Double Trouble

Graecinus, I remember you were sure
No man could fall in love with more than one
At the same time, and so I felt secure:
But you were wrong – that's just what I have done.

They both are beauties, both know how to dress,
Both are artistic, both I do adore,
But which of them excels in loveliness
I know not, nor which pleases me the more.

Just like a ship by inverse winds beset
I go from one to t'other, torn in twain
By each in turn. Why, Venus, do you let
Me suffer such a double share of pain?

Doesn't one girl sufficient care supply?
What need of further leaves has any tree?
Why set more stars into a crowded sky?
Why pour more water on the deep blue sea?

But all the same, I reckon that it is
Better to have two loves than sleep alone:
That's something I should wish my enemies,
To have to live austerely on one's own.

Unbridled love may interrupt my rest,
But better that than not to share a bed:
Of health and wealth may I be dispossessed
If not by one, then by two girls instead.

I've strength enough, although my stature's slight,
I'm short on weight, but not on stamina:
I'll pass the test of any girl who might
Elect to serve as love's examiner.

Pleasure will feed desire and make me strong:
How often have I whiled the hours away
In amorous encounters all night long,
Yet fighting fit when came the break of day!

Happy is he that draws his final breath
In such engagements: may it be my fate
In that same way, please God, to meet my death,
Unlike the fighting man, who has to wait

For enemies with swords to strike him down
And buys eternal glory with his blood,
Or greedy merchant venturers, who drown
At sea, their lying stifled by the flood.

No, not for me to die in such a fashion:
May Venus be more merciful, and send
A better death, when palpitating passion
Brings love, and also living, to an end.

Then someone, in my funeral oration,
May find some words of comfort he can give
Amid the mourners' cries of lamentation –
'He chose to die just as he chose to live.'

Amores, II, 10

Dawn

Now golden dawn appears above the sea,
Whose frosty chariot brings the light of day.
But why the haste, Aurora? Wait awhile,
For now's the very time I love to lie
Enfolded in my darling's soft embrace,
Now best of all the moment to enjoy
Our link of love, for now the air is chill
And sleep is cosy, and the little throats
Of birds pour forth their symphony of song.
Why then the haste, when neither man nor maid
Will bid you welcome? Let your rosy hands
Slacken the dewy reins. Before you rise
The sailor better steers his starlight course
Instead of drifting aimlessly at sea,
And when you come the weary traveller
Must wake, the soldier gird himself for war.
You are the first to watch the farmer till
His acres with the hoe, the first to call
The lazy ox beneath his crooked yoke;
'Tis your deceit betrays the sleepy boy
Whose tender hands must feel the master's cane;
'Tis you, when woman might enjoy a rest,
Who calls her daily to her loom again.
All things I could allow, but who could make
A girl get out of bed when morning comes,
Except the man who doesn't have a girl?

Amores, I, 13

No Admission

You whom they keep inhumanly in chains to guard the door,
Come on, just open up for me a moment, I implore:
It isn't much I'm asking, the merest chink will do,
For Love has made me slim enough to squeeze my body
      through.
No matter what the obstacles by which my path is barred,
Love shows my feet the way to slip unnoticed past the guard.

91

The thought of ghosties in the dark once gave me such a fright
I marvelled at the folk who dared to venture out at night:
Then Cupid with his mother whispered softly in my ear
And laughingly assured me he would rid me of my fear.
Along came Love, and now the nights no longer cause alarm,
I fear no more that spooky hands may clutch me by the arm.
Now it is *you* I fear, because your slowness could destroy me,
It's you I have to butter up, whose sluggish ways annoy me:
Draw back those cruel bolts, and you will see, you sleepyhead,
Those precious doors of yours are wet with tears that I have
    shed.
Don't you remember, one day when your mistress had you
    stripped,
I interceded with her that you should not be whipped?
It's shameful that you will not now do something to repay
Your kindly benefactor, who saved your skin that day.
If you returned the favour, you might get something more:
The night is getting shorter, so unbolt that ruddy door!
Unbolt it and, who knows, you might just find a grateful friend
To sever those long chains of yours, and slavery would end.
Hey, porter! Are you listening, or just as hard to move
As these oak doors, whose bolts remain stuck fast within their
    groove?
I grant that cities under siege have need of such defence,
But when there's not a war on, such fears do not make sense.
If you shut lovers out like this, whatever is in store
For enemies? The night slips by, unbolt that ruddy door!
I haven't got a military escort here with me,
I'm all alone except for Love, who keeps me company:
To part with him is something that I couldn't bear to do,
For if I ever did, I'd have to cut myself in two.
Yes, Love is my companion, with some wine, and on my pate
(A little damp) a garland which I fear is none too straight.
There's nothing to be frightened of, and as I've said before,
The night is getting shorter, so unbolt that ruddy door!
Are you asleep, you porter? And has my every word
Gone with the wind, you dim-wit, unheeded and unheard?
At other times when I have tried before to tiptoe past you
I've found you wide awake enough at well past midnight, blast
    you!

Maybe you've got a girl friend there to share your hours of
  rest?
If so, you lucky dog, I know I've come off second best:
To have my girl beside me, I'd even opt for your
Poor fettered state. It's getting late – unbolt that ruddy door!

Hark! Wasn't that a squeak I heard of hinges swinging round?
And didn't something shake the door and make a hollow
  sound?
But no, I'm wrong, for that was just a gust of wind that hit
Those stubborn doors, and blew away my fading hopes with
  it.
The silent city's shining wet with dew: there's little more
Of night to come, so hurry up, unbolt that ruddy door,
Or else this iron torch of mine will use its load of fire
To conflagrate this stately home and light its funeral pyre.
Night, Love and Wine all urge extremes, Night has no sense
  of shame:
As for the gods of Love and Wine, they're not afraid of flame.
I've begged you and I've threatened you – in vain, for you have
  stayed
Hard-hearted as the stoutest oak of which these doors are
  made:
For you to guard a pretty girl is not the right employment,
A job as prison gaoler would provide much more enjoyment.
Now Lucifer, the morning star, appears, to set in train
Dawn's frosty chariot, and the cock awakens once again
The wretched workers: so, you wreath, with which I have been
  crowned
All night, I'll tear you off my head and cast you on the ground,
So that later in the morning, when my lady sees you there,
She will know how long I waited with you garlanding my hair.
And now the time has come for me politely just to say
Goodbye to one and all of you as I go on my way:
Goodbye, you slowcoach, and your friends who joined you to
  deny
My entrance – doorpost, door and steps – I bid you all
  Goodbye.

Amores, I, 6

93

Martial

Martial (M. Valerius Martialis) was born in Spain in AD 43. He came to Rome at the age of twenty-three, and lived there for thirty-five years before returning to his birthplace for the last few years of his life. He acquired a considerable reputation for his satirical and often scurrilous comments on contemporary Roman life, and his poems were in demand throughout the empire, including Britain. He obtained the patronage of the emperors Titus and Domitian, to whom he showed a servile adulation hardly justified by their character and achievement.

Blood and Water

Where the Vipsanian column's neighbouring gate
Drips constant damp upon the slimy stone,
A pointed icicle with frozen weight
Fell, and pierced deep the youthful throat of one
Who passed beneath. Ah, cruel, cruel Fate,
To what fresh miracles will you conspire?
The warmth of blood dissolved the brittle blade:
The fatal weapon melted in the fire
Of that same wound which by itself was made.
If water can cut throats, what is Life's power?

IV, 18

Wise Poet

Two hundred lines of poetry you write,
Varus, of which not one will you recite:
The shafts of inspiration are so few,
I can but say, you fool, how wise of you.

VIII, 20

Unnatural Causes

Thais's teeth are black as jet,
    Laecania's pearly white:
The one still has her native set,
    The other – well, not quite.

                    V, 43

Trifling Request

You say it's nothing that you ask, you rascal. In reply you
May rest assured, dear Cinna, nothing's what I will deny you.

                    III, 61

Man About Town

'Oh, Algernon, so many say
    You're such a bright young spark;
Now tell me what this means, I pray:
    Don't keep me in the dark.'

'A 'spark' is one whose crinkled hairs
    Are kept in place with lotion,
Who drowns each garment that he wears
    In quite a scented ocean.
He whistles with supreme delight
    The continental hits;
He hits the high spots every night,
    And all day long he sits
In idleness, and flirts around
    With any girl who's near;
He whispers all that he has found
    In everybody's ear.
No day goes by, but he is sent
    A score of billets doux,
And he returns the compliment
    By writing not a few.

He shudders with a look of scorn
At any one whose dress
Is shabby and a little worn,
Or needs a wash-and-press.
He knows exactly who loves whom,
He's always out to dinner;
He's learned the sire of Golden Gloom
And every Derby winner.'

'Why, Algernon! Attend to me!
Are these of 'sparks' the features?
Then, Algernon, these 'sparks', I see,
Are pretty worthless creatures!'

III, 63

4-4=0

If rightly, Aelia, I recall,
You used to have four teeth in all;
You coughed, expelling half the four,
Then coughed again and lost two more:
Now cough as often as you choose
– You've no more ivories to lose.

I, 19

Recitation

I wonder why, when you recite,
A muffler round your neck appears?
I have a feeling that it might
Be better wrapped about our ears.

IV, 41

Unfair Exchange

This book, Pontilianus, that I write,
  Why don't I send it you? Because, you see,
Pontilianus, I'm afraid you might
  Reciprocate by sending yours to me.

VII, 3

Grand Vin?

A vintage consular in name
I drank tonight. You doubt my boast,
Asking how old, and whence it came?
Was it more generous than most?

The wine was bottled in the year
An ancient consul ruled in Rome:
I know, Severus, for I fear
I drank it at the consul's home.

VII, 79

Ringmaster

Six rings on every finger constantly
Charinus wears. Why, you may ask, won't he,
Going to bed, or just to wash his hands,
Ever remove those ornamental bands?
He hasn't got a box for them, you see.

XI, 59

Black and White

Cinna, your toga's like a coal-black sheet,
And yet your shoes are white as virgin snow:
Why then, poor fool, must you conceal your feet
And let that filthy toga hang so low?
Just hitch it up – then, as you walk the street,
It will allow your nice clean shoes to show.

VII, 33

Visitors Welcome?

I wasn't well – you came without delay
And brought a hundred pupils. On that day
A hundred icy hands caressed my brow:
I had no fever, Symmachus, till now.

V, 9

Hadrian

Unlike most Roman emperors, Hadrian, who ruled from 117-138 AD, was a scholar of distinction and a patron of the arts. He was the author of many works in verse and prose, of which unfortunately only a few Greek and Latin epigrams have survived. This delightful piece of soul-searching is the best-known example.

Body and Soul

My restless, gentle little soul,
So long my body's guest and friend,
Now that your sojourn nears its end
What land uncharted is your goal?
What sunless, chill and bleak hereafter
Is soon to rob me of your laughter?

Juvenal

The exact dates of Juvenal's life are uncertain, but we know that he was a contemporary of Martial, whom he survived by some years. He wrote his famous Satires during the early part of the second century AD, and although his verses, unlike those of Lucretius, are not notable for any great poetic brilliance, they make interesting and enjoyable reading, not least for the light they shed on daily life in the Rome of his day. In this third Satire, Juvenal humorously but mercilessly exposes the seamier side of the capital, and the horrors endured by those who lived there – vice, squalor, poverty, corruption and danger. Much of this is a recognisable anticipation of urban life in our own times, only too familiar to us, as it was to Dr Johnson, who in 1738 published his *London, a Poem in Imitation of the Third Satire of Juvenal*. The following are selected extracts.

Town and Country

Upsetting though it is to see a friend
Depart, I must wholeheartedly approve
His choice of Cumae[1] as a place to live:
The Sibyl[2] now will gain a citizen.
With Baiae[3] close at hand it is indeed
A pleasant spot upon a pretty coast.
Myself, I would prefer a desert isle
To Roman high street – bare or desolate,
One surely could not find it any worse
Than living always with the dread of fire
Or falling buildings, and the myriad
Of other perils in this cruel town,
And poets who defile the summer months
With endless recitations of their works.

My friend Umbricius said, 'There's not a chance
In Rome for any gain from honest toil.
My revenue has shrunk since yesterday,
And by tomorrow will have shrunk still more:
So I am off to where old Daedalus[4]
Laid down his weary wings, while still my hair
Is hardly grey, and I am not too old
To stand upright, and need no walking stick
To prop me up, and while the hand of Fate
Has not yet spun away my thread of life.
So I'm retiring, leaving Rome to those
In whose eyes black is white, and who obtain
All kinds of contracts – for construction schemes
Of temples, river dredging, harbour works,
Sewage or funerals, and then sell up
Their property in bogus bankruptcy.
Once they blew horns, these men, always on hand
In local theatres, with their puffed-out cheeks
A common sight; but now they put on shows
Themselves, and when the people's signal is
Thumbs Down, they kill to popular acclaim,
Then build a lot of public lavatories.
Why stop at that, when these are humble men
Whom Fortune, if she wants to have a laugh,
Lifts from the gutter up to dizzy heights?

Now let me tell of that unpleasant race
Beloved of all our richest citizens,
Which above all I shun: I'll not disguise
My loathing for the Greek community.
And yet of all that urban excrement
How many can be reckoned truly Greek?
Orontes[5] has for years disgorged its flood
Into our river Tiber, bringing us
An unfamiliar tongue and mode of life –
Strange kinds of harps, and flutes and tambourines,
And girls on offer at the Hippodrome
(That's where you'll find the foreign prostitutes
Who wear those brightly painted headdresses).

Don't blame me if I choose to run away
From all these purple-garment immigrants
Whose signatures appear above my own,
And who at dinner parties can expect
A better seat than mine: these men blow in
With damson imports and a load of figs.
Does it mean nothing that in infancy
I breathed the air of Rome, my nourishment
Derived from Sabine olives? And besides,
These men are all accomplished flatterers,
Praising what ignoramuses may say
And telling ugly friends how nice they look.
A weakling with a neck that's much too long
They call a Hercules who's strong enough
To lift Antaeus[6] high above the ground:
They wax ecstatic when they hear a voice
So shrill that one might justly liken it
To cackling hen that's bitten by a cock.
We too are free to pay such compliments,
But theirs are thought sincere. And on the stage
There's no one better in a comedy
To play a female role – a courtesan,
An honourable lady or a maid –
Without the need for a concealing cloak:
You'd think it was a woman, and not just
An actor who's dependent on a mask.

The Greek's a natural actor. If you laugh
He laughs enough to split his sides, but if
A friend is seen to cry, his tears pour down,
Although he feels no real sympathy.
Ask for a fire when it's a chilly day,
And he'll at once put on his overcoat:
Tell him you're hot, and he will start to sweat;
At any time of night or day he can
Match his expression to the circumstance –
Throw up his hands, or clap them when he hears
A friend produce a satisfying belch.
I can't compete with such accomplishments.

In court, these days, the mere integrity
Of witnesses is thought of no account:
What matters is their wealth. "How many slaves
Has he? How many acres of his land?
How many dinner plates does he possess,
And are they porcelain?" Each man's good faith
Is measured by the money in his safe.
Whatever gods the poor man may elect
To swear by, he'll be deemed a perjuror
Defying heaven's thunderbolts, although
The gods themselves may pardon his untruth.
He'll be the constant butt for many jests
Because his filthy topcoat's badly torn,
Or if his toga has a spot of dirt,
Or else the leather on one shoe is split,
Or if a scar betrays that more than once
The coarse material has been repaired.
There's nothing harder for the poor to bear
Than being made to look ridiculous.
"For shame," says someone, "he must leave at once
And quit that cushioned seat reserved for knights
If he has not sufficient property
To meet the law's requirements." These are seats
Which sons of panders occupy, who were
Begotten in some brothel. In this place
The offspring of some glossy auctioneer
May clap his hands, surrounded by his gang
Of youthful dandies, gladiators' sons
And sons of those who train them. This is what
Those rules on theatre seats have brought about.
Who would approve a man for son-in-law
Unless he had sufficient worldly goods
To match his daughter's dowry? What poor man
Is ever made the heir in any will,
Or picked to fill the humblest civil post?
All citizens of slender means long since
Should have formed fours and quitted Rome for good.
However talented a man may be,
It's difficult for him to make his mark
Without some private means, but here in Rome

It's harder still. Such hospitality
As you provide, however scant it is,
Costs you a packet, as it does to feed
Your slaves, or have a modest meal yourself.
You feel ashamed to dine off earthenware,
And yet you wouldn't mind if suddenly
Transported to some rural dining room,
Content to sup in rough blue overalls.
To tell the truth, in much of Italy
The toga's worn by few until they die:
Even at festival performances
In grassy theatres, when some well-known farce
At last is being tardily revived,
And peasant children on their mothers' laps
Are frightened by the actor's gaping mask,
The audience, from balcony to stalls,
All dress alike: even the magistrates
Think a white tunic will suffice to be
The outward evidence of dignity.
But here in Rome it's quite beyond one's means
To tog oneself in fancy clothes: the most
That one can do is, every now and then,
To borrow from the wardrobe of a friend.
That is the universal trouble here –
Pretentious poverty is what we all
Endure. Why now prolong my tale of woe?
In Rome there is a price for everything.

No countryman need fear, or ever has,
The imminent collapse of his abode
In cool Praeneste[7] or in Tivoli,
Perched on its hillside, but our city is
Largely propped up by feeble buttresses:
That's how the agent, though the house is close
To falling down, just keeps it standing up
And, papering the cracks in ancient walls,
Assures the tenant he can sleep secure.
Better to live where there's no risk of fire,
No fear at night. "Water!" your neighbour shouts,
Moving his odds and ends into the street,

While you yourself have not the least idea
Your upper rooms are going up in smoke;
For if the alarm is given down below,
The chap whose sole protection from the rain
Is just the roof, up on the attic floor,
Where pigeons nest, will be the last to fry.
The poor man loses everything he has,
Which isn't much: to make things even worse,
He goes about in rags to beg a crust,
For none will give the wretched man a meal
Or shelter. But when homes of wealthy men
Suffer destruction, women rend their hair,
Nobles wear black and law-courts are adjourned:
Then we bewail the risks of life in Rome,
Proclaiming fire our deadly enemy.
While yet the house is burning, someone hastes
To offer gifts of marble, or to make
A contribution to the owner's costs:
Here comes a statue of some naked nymph,
Maybe a bronze from some Greek sculptor's hand,
Or relics from an oriental shrine,
Bookcases, books, Minerva's bust, or else
A heap of silver. Thus does Persicus[8],
The most distinguished of the destitute,
Replace his losses with still better things,
And more of them, while some may well suspect
It was the owner's hand that fired the house.

If you can bear to tear yourself away
From circus races, buy a country house –
It will not cost you more than you might pay
To rent some dismal hovel for a year.
There is a little garden, and a well
Whence water can be hauled up easily
To keep your tender cuttings nice and moist.
You'll find you will enjoy your gardening,
Plying the hoe and nurturing a crop
That could provide a vegetarian feast.
Wherever you are, no matter how remote,
It's something to possess your own estate

And give a single lizard tenancy.
Here in the city most inhabitants
Die of insomnia, health is undermined
By ill-digested food and stomach pains.
I ask you, how can anyone contrive
To sleep in lodgings? Here the rich alone
Enjoy a good night's rest, and illness comes
From sleeplessness. Those blasted carriages
Rumbling along the narrow winding streets,
The shouts of those caught up in traffic jams,
Would wreck the sleepiest emperor's[9] repose.
And there are other dangers of the night
To be remembered. Think from what a height
Those falling tiles can penetrate your skull,
How often all those cracked and broken pots
Are hurled from windows – just see how their weight
Can smash the pavement. You're improvident,
Careless of accidents, unless you make
Your will before you venture out to dine:
Each open window there above your head
Is fraught with danger. So you'd better pray
That nothing worse descends upon your pate
Than just a harmless basinful of slops.

Many another reason could I give
For leaving Rome, but now the animals
Are telling me it's time that I was off:
The sun is setting, and the muleteer
Has long been making signals with his whip.
And so, goodbye to you. Remember me,
And any time you're leaving Rome yourself
To hasten to the country for a rest,
I'll gladly leave my seaside home awhile,
And, putting on my stoutest pair of shoes,
Pay you a visit on your cold estate[10].
If I deserve it, you can read to me
The latest book of *Satires* from your pen.'

Satires, III

NOTES:
1. The oldest Greek colony in Italy, on the Campanian coast.
2. The ageless prophetess who lived in a cave at Cumae.
3. A popular Roman seaside resort, akin to our Brighton.
4. Father of Icarus and mythological pioneer of human flight. According to legend, he landed at Cumae after his flight from Crete.
5. The principal river of Syria.
6. An African giant, invincible as long as he stayed in contact with the ground. Hercules lifted him up and strangled him.
7. The modern Palestrina.
8. Presumably a well-known, wealthy citizen.
9. This may refer to the emperor Claudius (T. Claudius Drusus) whose tendency to somnolence was proverbial.
10. Aquinum, Juvenal's birthplace.